Dear Pam,

Thank you for all your help and encouragment! I you enjoy it.

Let me know - think either by phone, email will meet for drinks and talk!

Your friend
Robin

860-989-9400
rvw1235711@hotmail.com

Five Hundred Miles From Help

And I Heard...

ROBIN WAITE

Contents

PART 2

Thank you Pat Wagner,
for all the years of friendship we have shared,
for the thousands of hours of prayer you have prayed,
and for your mentorship in things of the spirit.

PREFACE

This book tells the story of a physical crisis caused by life-threatening illness and the challenges of the body, mind, and spirit during the process of healing. The story alternates between the physical realm and the more esoteric realm of the spirit. The form of the book is reminiscent of ABAB—known as binary form in musical composition.

Modulation in music can occur in many ways: a common chord, closely related keys, or a common melody. For more radical changes, something as simple as one common note can be used to completely alter a key or an entire composition.

Robin Waite uses sleep, an image, or even a word as a modulation or pivot point to move from the physical and logical world to the more spiritual representations she presents. She brings us along on her journey in a lyrical style reminiscent of song. Her use of language flows like a river.

For those unfamiliar with musical terminology, a glossary can be found in the back of the book.

Introduction

As a Christian for many years, I studied the Bible, went to church, and practiced what was preached to me. I believed the Word and did all I could to walk according to its instruction.

One day, I was suddenly placed in a life-threatening situation over which I had absolutely no control. I was out to sea, five hundred miles from any semblance of help when I was struck by symptoms of a life-threatening illness. I had no choice but to depend upon God for my life.

This book tells the story of my journey from near-death, through fear and darkness in the middle of the Atlantic Ocean, to a place of trust and healing. I learned how to fight for healing and restoration using my body, mind, and spirit. I depended upon God and came through my experience with grace. Like Job, I was able to say after my ordeal, "I have heard of You by the hearing of the ear, but now my eyes see You." (Job, Chpt. 42:5 Bible, New King James Version)

God accompanied me into troubled waters and through the valley of the shadow of death. All the while, He was with me to help. He never left my side. This story chronicles our adventure.

"I would have lost heart unless I had believed." (Ps. 27: 13)

PSALM 23

A Psalm of David

1 The Lord is my shepherd; I shall not want.
2 He maketh me to lie down in green pastures:
He leadeth me beside the still waters.
3 He restoreth my soul: He leadeth me in the
paths of righteousness for His name's sake.
4 Yea, though I walk through the valley of the shadow
of death, I will fear no evil: for thou art with me;
thy rod and thy staff, they comfort me.
5 Thou preparest a table before me in the presence of mine
enemies: Thou anointest my head with oil; my cup runneth over.
6 Surely goodness and mercy shall follow me all the days of
my life: and I will dwell in the house of the Lord forever.

"THE WATER WALKER"

Wild seas surround, breathing, heaving.
The decks and the rigging, slanting, screaming.
Nothing is solid, nothing is fixed.
Salt stings like needles, no horizon exists.
Vibrating atmosphere bolted with power
rattles the core of the terrified travelers.
Breathing shallow.
Panting quick.
Chest constricting.
Stomach sick.
No way forward.
Can't go back.
Panic stalks.
Fear attacks.
Legs of butter.
Feet of clay.
Praying for the light of day.
Hope is waning.
Courage fled. Eyes look up.
Is this the end?
Then—a light in the distance. An apparition, a ghost?
No. A query, an answer, astonishment ... What?
A still quiet voice through the dark maelstrom floats.
"Fear not. I am with you. Get out of the boat."

PART 1

THE SHIP

I was going up that gangway to board the ship even if I had to crawl. I was ready to go to beautiful Bermuda—one of the most remote islands in the Atlantic—ready to flourish and heal in a place where beauty fills the senses. I thought I was ready for anything.

Instead, I began a journey I would never have chosen to take: an unexpected sojourn into a strange and unknown country. A journey into and through the valley of the shadow of death.

I'd received a diagnosis of diverticulosis, what I'd thought was an innocuous illness. For years I had been plagued with "tummy" troubles: pain, swelling, general discomfort, sensitivity to certain types of foods, and an occasional fever when infection flared. It was annoying to me and to those around me. I constantly experimented by abstaining from various foods. Doctors were unsure of how to avoid the problems I faced. I was frustrated by the guesswork and was willing to do anything to avoid the misery the illness caused.

When infection flared, doctors prescribed antibiotics. The drugs worked until the next flare-up. The medication's name— antibiotic —should have clued me into the seriousness of the matter: an antibiotic against life. My illness had exactly that in store for me: an attack against life. The threat was closer and more powerful than anything I could've imagined.

Before traveling to Bermuda, my diverticulosis flared into an infection. This was perhaps the third or fourth time a flare-up had resulted in infection. I visited the emergency room, received a cat scan, and was given a diagnosis of infection. Antibiotics had worked to tame infections in the past, so I continued with plans to cruise to Bermuda for a week's respite.

I thought the week would bring relaxation, eating, and merrymaking. I packed everything I thought I needed for any contingency. I brought antibiotics, probiotics, laxatives, antidiarrheal medication, and yes, even my much-dreaded enema. I was all set. Surely everything would be fine.

Of course, hindsight paints a clearer picture. I was not aware of the ticking time bomb within my body. I should have never gone.

Instead of merrymaking, eating, and relaxing, I spent the week drinking water and broth, and fighting nausea, exhaustion, and intestinal paralysis. My instincts warned me that something was seriously wrong. I knew—without consciously knowing—that my life was threatened. The nearest emergency help entailed a helicopter trip back to the United States from our location in the middle of the Atlantic.

One afternoon, after a long sleep, I arose from my sickbed and knew I was in serious trouble—life-threatening trouble. My abdomen was monstrously distended, and I was experiencing a distinct pain I'd never experienced before. If my intestines exploded, as they do in some cases, I would have lasted only a few minutes before perishing. There would be no time for helicopter transport. I knew all my efforts to prepare for the worst were not going to be enough. I knew that my only hope was going to be in the one I call the Lord of my life. I stood up, placed my hands on my sore, swollen belly, and whispered to Him, "Father, I am in serious trouble. I feel it. Only You can help. Please heal me."

It was a quiet but desperate call, one drawn from need, absolute dependence, and trust. Deep called unto deep. (New King James Version Ps. 42:7) I felt His two hands within me. They encircled and held my wounded intestines. And I heard His response in the still, small voice I have come to recognize and trust.

"Robin, I will heal you."

I marveled. He had called me by name.

The ship returned to port a day later. I felt sicker than ever before. Surely my gut was close to exploding. On the drive home from the ship, I had to hold myself so bouncing car would not jar me and cause disaster.

After arriving home, I was transported to the emergency room again. After a couple hours of observation and tests, I was admitted to the hospital for more intense treatment. The doctors were going to deliver antibiotics through an intravenous needle.

Back at home, I reluctantly but quickly packed my bag and was driven to the hospital to begin my unexpected, unwelcome adventure.

A Simple Hike

The hike I had planned was about ten miles up and back. It led to a trail that ran above a valley cut into the mountainside by a river. I loaded my pack and set off on my adventure. It seemed like an interesting place to explore. I had no intention of climbing down into the gorge. A look from the rim would satisfy my curiosity.

I ventured upward. As the morning progressed, the trail became steeper, tougher than I had imagined. I struggled to gain my footing. The rock became like shale, sharp and slippery. I was almost to the top and did not want to retreat after all this work, so I made one last slithering effort to gain the high trail which overlooked the chasm.

The trail ran beside the cliff. The terrain was not difficult, but alongside it steep walls fell away into the shadows below. Fascinated by the ominous view, I stared into the depths of the chasm—so different from the sunny shelf on which I traveled. I made a mental note to take great care not to trip and fall.

Details were obscured. Much of the valley was cast in shadow, some places deeper than others. The stone walls were steep and slick from the rising mists of the river far below. Boulders and rock shelves jutted outward, obscuring the view. The distant sound of wild water echoed as it zigzagged its way upward from the depths. As I walked above it, I looked down and imagined with trepidation what it might be like to travel through it.

Shadows passed over the mountain above me. It was time to turn back. The sun had begun its descent toward the horizon. It was not a good idea to be out here after dark. As I turned, I noticed that black, boiling cumulonimbus clouds had gathered behind me. They had developed quickly and had been spread by the jet stream into dark anvil shapes. Ugly weather was coming.

I quick-stepped back toward the point I had arrived at, near the upper trail. Lightning was a serious threat at any time—but at this elevation, even more so. As I approached the trail to descend, running water began to collect and swirl around my feet. I looked ahead. Retracing my steps was no longer possible. A storm had washed out the trail. The trail was now a river. The dirt and shale through which I had ascended had become a rushing river of debris and razor-sharp rocks. In this part of the country, weather was unpredictable. It took shape in micro-climatic patterns. One part of the trail could be bathed in sunlight while another, just around a bend, was simultaneously being ravaged by rain and storm. My return home was blocked. I was forced to turn around to find another way down.

As I searched for an alternative route, the trail became more arduous. Stones and boulders replaced the relatively flat terrain. I had to scramble over boulders larger than houses or crawl below them on hands and knees. The sound of the distant water reminded me of the vista below. The obstacles in my way obstructed my view.

❁

ARRIVAL

I was hooked up to an IV upon arriving in my hospital room. Nurses loved to fill me with fluids, and soon I was a human water balloon who traveled to the bathroom every twenty minutes. Normally it would not have been a problem, but I was forced to trail the unwieldy intravenous stand with me wherever I went. I named her Phyllis.

Phyllis was a six-legged, tree-like individual who stood straight and tall. From her trunk sprouted four hooked branches. From those branches hung various bags—fruits in the form of prescribed fluids and medications.

Phyllis had a powerful personality and loved to dance. She was not a good follower. She spun around at will. With each step, she ran and bounced over bare toes. She nipped at heels with her substantial, twirling, undisciplined bulk. Phyllis was tied to the wall with a relatively short cord, from which she drew her limited power. That cord, of course, did not stretch into the bathroom. As she spun, the cord wound around her thin trunk and further limited our travel distance. She was attached behind the bed, far out of the reach. Before every sojourn to the bathroom, she had to be detached. I had to reach behind the bed—beyond several other contraptions that filled the space—to loosen her bonds.

Phyllis, efficient as she was, was handicapped with a severely limited battery life. She had a vocal personality and, like a crowing rooster in the early morning, she made her needs known without apology. Her energy was drained with an annoying nasally voice that beeped or whined to signal her impatience. It was impossible to shut her up for long without the assistance of a nurse—one I had to wait for. Phyllis also beeped to draw attention to her empty IV bag, to warn those in charge that medication had been completely dispensed, or, like a spoiled and hungry child, to complain of a low battery.

Those in charge were never within earshot. I had to ring an additional bell for a nurse. Phyllis' demands were not intermittent. She beeped and crowed nonstop until her computer could be reset by authorized medical personnel. Her irritating calls rang out any time—day or night, even when her patient was sound asleep.

Back and forth we went. To the bathroom. Up, down, and around the halls. Wherever we ventured, my annoying companion accompanied me relentlessly. I was not allowed outdoors into the beautiful May sunshine. Access to outside was not permitted without supervision. For three days, I waited and watched from my fifth-floor window as the world whizzed by—a world completely unaware of the suffering hidden behind our walls. For three days, I was a prisoner within those walls, chained to Phyllis.

After a constant flow of antibiotics into my veins—seventy-two hours, standard protocol—I had not improved at all. I was shocked, especially considering my history of success with medication. There I sat in my comfortable non-hospital clothes, expecting release at any moment. I looked to my doctor, who stood in the far corner of my room.

"Well," he said calmly, "we're going to have to operate."

My eyes fired a salvo of shock over his shoulder into the saucer-wide stare of my friend. I was struck with mind numbing terror, completely unable to process the word "operate."

The doctor had informed me that he would have to slice me open to fix a problem that I'd thought, just five minutes earlier, could be solved by swallowing a few pills. My stomach sank.

My mind went blank. But there were eyes beyond my doctor's shoulders that veiled their initial shock and gazed back at me with confidence and solidity. They became my initial calming influence.

With my surgeon's few words, my path turned on a dime. The sunny, carefree trail on which I walked instantly became a treacherous path. My unexpected, unwelcome journey into the darkest valley of my life had begun.

GRAVITY

As I hiked down my alternative route, the grade began to descend. I was struck with a mild foreboding. I wanted to go down, but this trail led me in the wrong direction. It dropped gently at first, then suddenly steepened and tipped down toward the canyon.

I stopped. I could move forward or return from where I had just come. I chose to continue. My options were limited. I stepped tentatively.

Not tentatively enough. Suddenly my feet shot skyward. I fell backward, sliding on the gravelly mix beneath my back. The grade steepened as I slipped downward. My skin scraped raw against gravel, briers, and sharp rocks. I scrabbled for a hold, but one handful of stone after another gave way and crumbled to dust in my bleeding palms. After a quick and painful slide, I slowed. For a moment, as I teetered upon the precipitous edge, I hoped that I could stop. My legs dangled over the edge.

I watched from outside my body as I struggled to prevent myself from slipping into the void. The inexorable force of gravity took me—as if a hand had reached out to grab me from below—and yanked me over the edge.

Uh Oh

The conversation with my surgeon informed me of the processes, and the waiting began. I was set to go in for surgery that night or the next morning. Shock reverberated within my entire body. It took time—more time than I had then—to come to grips with what awaited me. The longer I waited, the more the unknown pressed its ugly face into my imagination. It contorted itself into grotesque forms, like a face pressed against distorted glass.

The nurses and aides had previously *suggested* I wear hospital-issued clothing, and I'd declined. But now they insisted I don the official vestments of illness. I had resisted them for three days. In fact, one of my nurses told me I had resisted longer and more vehemently than any patient she'd ever had. Wearing my own comfortable clothes distanced me. It separated me from the idea that I was ill and headed for something I could not yet imagine. But with the donning of the dreaded johnny gown, I became a member of the hospital population. It was official. My journey had begun. I did not want to go, but I had to.

My doctor scheduled a test so he could have a quick "look-see" at me. He wanted more detail before I underwent surgery. I waited in my room for the nice young man whose full-time job it was to push patients around the hospital to their destinations. I hadn't previously been aware of all the routes within the hospital. My conversation with him taught me much about his responsibilities.

Each conveyance posed its own special challenges—both
for the pusher and the pushee. I witnessed one young man
negotiate an entire hospital bed into an elevator with a "K" turn
from an impossibly narrow hallway. He dodged a misplaced
food delivery cart without jostling his groaning passenger. The
feat required skill and practice. Another adventure involved
transporting my oversized wheelchair. It was broad enough to
accommodate three of me, and the footrests far outstretched my
inseam. The chair, powered by my energetic chauffeur, traveled
at light speed. Woe be unto the errant foot that, without care,
could become snagged on corners or become an effective, if
painful, wheelchair bola.

As we whizzed through the hallways the freezing, air-
conditioned breeze whipped through my hair. But the excitement
of the trip was unfortunately not sufficient to erase the thoughts
lodged in my imagination.

We arrived at our destination. My chauffeur left me with a
breezy goodbye. He wished me good luck first, and then I was
left sitting in the hall accompanied only by my johnny and my
panicky thoughts. Next to me, beyond a partially pulled divider,
poked a pair of calloused feet topped by fungus infested toenails.
Attached to them were bandaged, spiny, anonymous legs that
stretched out from insufficient cover on their frozen gurney.

I sat there quaking with fear and cold. Those legs looked like
they belonged in a morgue. Finally, they were wheeled away to an
unknown destination. This was the hall for testing, for waiting.
We were waiting to be "done unto"—a feeling I was about to
become well acquainted with.

The testers arrived. They rolled me efficiently into the room.
A metal gurney with plenty of padding dominated the space. The
table was perfectly set with pillow and tablecloth. Above it, from
a shiny metal rack, hung a bag the size and shape of a grown cow's
udder. It made a most hideous chandelier. The blazing, uninviting

lights illuminated the space with the strength of the sun. The operators of the space sat waiting behind a protective glass.

"Hello," they smiled. They were nice, brimming with empathy. Why? What was coming? It must be horrible, I thought. I sat there immersed in dread. Tears began to drip silently from my sealed eyes.

There was a delay. I was forced to wait for twenty minutes while my imagination clawed at my emotions. I thought about that immense volume of fluid being forced into places it did not belong. I was in pain already. What was this going to do to me? I sensed in the quiet depths within me that it would be lethal. I waited. The rolling tears became a flood. My instinct transmitted serious warning.

They propped me upon the table like a human sacrifice. I lay there freezing—the staff kept these rooms cold like a morgue. Everything was ready and waiting. The bag-chandelier hung overhead, taunting me. It whispered to me that pain was on my horizon. I openly wept with fear. Twenty minutes passed.

Unbeknownst to me, my radiologist had been discussing the wisdom of this test with my surgeon during those twenty minutes. Apparently the radiologist who was to perform the test agreed with *me*. He called the operators of the room and informed all of us that he thought the test was too dangerous to perform on a person in my acute condition.

I had no proof. My instinct told me that this radiologist had probably saved me from serious, perhaps dire, consequences. At first, relief pulsed through me. But then the anger came. Why hadn't they discussed this before bringing me down to the torture chamber? I was reminded of a medieval torture museum I had visited in Germany. I remembered the rack, the iron maiden, and the various other creative devices used to inflict great pain and suffering on the slow road to death.

I was angry and traumatized. I could not control my weeping. It acted like a pressure release valve. Out flooded the tears and the tension.

They took me off the table, covered me up again in my johnny, and left me alone in the hall without privacy, exposed to all. I was mortified. I could not stop crying. I asked them to please put me behind a curtain, but they refused. They had to monitor my condition, they said. They left me sitting there in open humiliation.

I waited and wept. I wished desperately that I could curl into a ball and disappear. My humiliation enfolded me in a blanket of shame. I had been "done unto" against my will—stuck on the side of an ice-cold hallway like a piece of beaten chicken in a fridge. The absence of humanity and my complete lack of control combined to produce in me a feeling of living death.

I was psychologically tortured. As I waited, I thought about a strategy used by the Russians in their prisons. They would tell a filthy prisoner that he was to be released. He would shower, believing his family awaited him to take him home. When he was clean and ready to dress for release, they threw him his filthy clothes, laughed, and told him that they were just kidding. He wasn't being released, and no one was coming to save him. Prisoners were then forced to dress in their stinking vestments of captivity and were thrown back into prison. That was how I felt.

After too long a wait, my chauffeur arrived. My humiliation expanded down the whizzing halls like the billowing veil of a jilted bride. It followed me up the elevator and into my room. I was unceremoniously deposited there, left to my acerbic thoughts; just another lump of the population that awaited various fates.

Later, I was informed that the battle against my illness was to be engaged in the early afternoon the following day.

❁

Into the Theater

The next day dawned. Hospital routine had become my new normal. The nurse entered and piped, "Good morning, time for your blood clot shot."

"Do you have to put it into my sore belly again?"

"Yes."

"Any room for negotiation on placement?"

"No."

The shots burned and left nasty red reminders of their daily insults. I found myself counting their painful calling cards. One day, I counted fourteen.

There had been no food since my arrival four days previous. In fact, no food for the two weeks prior to my arrival. I had been unable to stomach anything, unable to even imagine eating. Only a menu of "Chips and Sips" had been allowed. That instruction was written efficiently upon the diminutive white board hanging on my wall. These were not the fun kind of chips I loved—the salty variety—but rather the cold crunch of tiny ice chased down with a drop of their finest water. My stomach was empty, ready for its roller coaster adventure.

While my stomach was prepared, my mind was not. I fought the queasiness of illness and the sick repetition of fear dropping in my gut. I began to fight the battle of the mind with thoughts of trust, and I was greeted by minute-by-minute reminders of the voice I'd heard as I stood by my bed in the middle of the Atlantic: "Robin, I will heal you."

The operating room nurse arrived to administer the large-bore surgical IV needle in my other arm. She was an expert: quick, efficient, and inflicted a minimum of pain. I thanked her. It was important to let her know how much I appreciated her skill.

I tended to talk to everyone. Ever the curious academic, I asked questions of all who came to help. I'd discovered the large-bore IV was necessary because of the amount of medicine that had to be flooded into my vein. Propofol—an extremely effective and delightful respite from pain and worry—was on the menu for the day. Having asked the doctor how it worked, I was informed that when administered properly it affected the brain like alcohol but with none of alcohol's negative side effects. (I.e., no hangover.)

The transport team arrived. They rolled me, bed and all, with zippy efficiency to my destination: a darkened room where I waited to be taken into the operating theater. I was reminded of the dim quiet of a darkened theater just before a suspenseful movie begins. Multiple patients waited with hushed anticipation in the lobby outside the operating theater. We were not excited; we were the audience and participants of an upcoming production who waited on high alert while our dreadful, orchestral thoughts prepared us for the worst.

The staff, to counteract what they knew was frightening to us, were kind and relaxed. Their demeanor was contagious, and I began to sense a calm spread throughout the room.

It did not take long for my journey to begin. They came to wheel me into the theater. This theater did not display the artistic lighting of Broadway. Instead, it was lit by two gigantic arrays of lights that hung above another perfectly set table.

The table was set with an intricate and far more complex display of tableware than those of any fancy dinner I'd ever attended. I estimated the candlepower of the chandelier was about one million.

As I arrived at the table, I spoke to my surgeon. I'd had him for another procedure a year ago and liked and trusted him. He took command of his surgical team like the captain of a great sailing vessel. His attitude possessed the perfect balance of command, confidence, and humor. He was confident enough to tell me not to worry—whatever problems they found he could fix. At the same time, he was never reckless. I respectfully called him Captain. His attitude suited me perfectly.

As I entered, I greeted him and made two requests. My first was that he would take a picture of what was removed. The second was that he weigh whatever he removed. He questioned me.

"Really?"

"Yes," I said. "I want to know how much weight has been removed so I can have an accurate weight loss measurement when all this is over." He laughed and said, "Sure." That was the sense of humor I appreciated.

"Who would you like me to call following the surgery?" he asked.

I gave him two names.

"I usually call only one person. But for you, I'll call both."

They transferred me expertly from the bed to the table. I'd become a human centerpiece, surrounded not by diners, but by staff whose business it was to save my life.

It was time to get down to that business. In my mind I played my familiar game: I tried to count backwards from 100 and make it past 95. And while I tried to feel the effects of the drugs taking hold gradually, I was not successful.

FALLING

I fell in slow motion and watched the jagged walls of the canyon slip by me. The sky overhead receded as I sank into the darkness below. As I tumbled, I imagined the hidden sounds behind the rock walls: the tapping, sighing, muffled whooshing. And the—wait, was that laughter?

I fell deeper into the abyss. A cold and dark river tumbled at the base of the cliff walls. I landed within its watery grasp, just barely missing the rocky bank at its edge by a few feet.

The current swept me into its embrace and carried me deeper into the gorge. The walls rose steeply above me. They grew higher and more forbidding with each passing breath. The current ran swiftly. Rapids broke over my head and prevented my lungs from breathing. Submerged rocks pummeled my legs and stabbed at my back and gut as I caromed down the rushing river. I lost consciousness.

Eventually, the current slowed and deposited me onto a muddy bank. I groggily awoke to find myself stuck on my back in six inches of thick muck. I lay upon the slippery, wet bank, bedraggled and gasping for air. I was cold, nauseous, and seriously wounded. As I lay still upon the ground, my eyes slowly opened. My blurred vision began to clear and, barely breathing, I took in my surroundings.

The wet walls of the canyon rose high above me into the darkening sky. Like impregnable castle walls, they soared into a low-gray ceiling. Their jagged battlements pierced the clouds, and rain began to fall. It came slowly at first, then, bit by bit, increased to a torrent that whipped against my shivering body.

Water poured from the sky. The river rushed by my heels resting on its bank. Its waves encroached upon my feet and ankles as it tried to pull me back into its cold, clammy death-grip. I struggled to turn over to drag myself up the riverbank. But I was unable to move. My pack dug into the mud like an anchor and held me fast.

Night descended. I lay helpless in the muck and prayed that the river would not reclaim me. Sleep finally overtook me, a blessed respite from my ordeal and from the troubling imaginations of what might come.

❁

REVELATIONS

I awoke after surgery and commented to the operating room staff, "That was quick."

My surgeon's laser focus found me through arched brows. He said,

"For you. For us, the operation was complicated and serious. Five hours have passed since we last spoke."

Five hours—in which time they'd worked to save my life. It was a foreshadowing of the fragmented revelations that would slowly reveal themselves as the days progressed. At that time, I was not aware of how closely death had drawn to my doorstep.

They wheeled me into recovery. I was euphoric to have missed the entire thing. Still groggy, I rocked in and out of sleep. Later, my body began to introduce me in excruciating detail to every move the surgeons had made while I'd slept, blissfully unaware.

Awakening

I awoke to a cold watery light that penetrated the canyon's gray drizzle. For a moment, I forgot where I was. It didn't take long to remember.

One effort to rise produced a stabbing reminder of the ordeal that had led me to my undignified arrival on this muddy riverbank. I urged my tired feet to stand, but they refused. The only parts of my body willing to function were my arms. I tried to sit up. My gut resisted the effort with searing pain, my back cried out in protest. I thought: I must have been brutally wounded in my tumble down the rapids.

My head flopped back onto the ground, where I took stock of my situation. I lay in the mud at the bottom of a deep valley. I could see no way out. I knew I could not remain there for long without suffering hypothermia and further injury. My pack remained on my back during my tumble through the water. I was grateful—it had anchored me to the riverbank during the night. I could not move on my own. But to get out of this valley, I had to find a way.

Though exhausted, I began to think. I'd set out on a simple hike. How had I ended up in these circumstances? It was sunny and easy the day before. What happened? My thoughts began to whine in my ear like the slow squeak of a rusty hinge. Thinking would get me nowhere. To make any progress, I had to adapt and put slow, small goals in front of me. I determined to crawl or drag myself forward in any way I could.

My priority was to distance myself from the volatile river. In these circumstances, it could rise in an instant and swallow me into an unknown darkness. I raised my arms above my head to feel for any handhold I could. As I blindly explored, my fingers touched the edge of a rock lodged in the mud. I stretched to reach it and grasp my fingers around any edge. With every move, the heat of pain tore through my gut, down into my hips, and up into my bruised rib cage. I moaned with each effort, the outbursts functioning like a pressure release valve. Finally, I pulled myself a few inches up the bank.

The pack that had anchored me the night before became an impediment to my progress. The mud resisted my efforts. All my life-saving gear had become, for the time being, excess baggage. I struggled to release it—no easy task considering the well-fitted straps and buckles.

Had it only been a day? I rested for a few minutes to let the pain ebb from my system.

❁

Accommodations

I arrived in my room a shadow of my previous self. The effects of the anesthesia had ebbed with increasingly unpleasant results. Hooked up to Phyllis once again, I noticed that a new bag of antibiotics drained into a tributary to join the river of saline. From another tributary, the drip of morphine invited relief from the emerging consequences of surgery. By now I had become a true member of the population. I saw my johnny differently than I had the previous day. My focus was no longer on the discomfort and awkwardness of the garment. Rather, I saw it as an absolute necessity. It provided access for the additional tubes and doubled as a disposable drop cloth for the various fluids leaking from my body.

I lay awkwardly on my back at the bottom of an incline. The head of the bed had been steeply elevated (hospital beds are amazingly adjustable—the possibilities for movement limited only by the imagination). I was fortunate no other weird machinations had occurred. Apparently, I had slipped to the bottom as I slept. My chest made an unnatural resting place for my chin. I reached blindly above my head to grab a hold of anything I could. I found a secure handrail and dragged myself incrementally up the incline. I was grateful for all the hours of swimming that had given me the strength to do so.

From my new vantage point on the bed, I gazed down at the brand-new ileostomy bag, an alien attached to my right side. This piece of equipment was affectionately nicknamed the "exit

29

ramp" by my surgeon. Its purpose was to divert the flow of waste to the outside of my body before it traveled to the newly repaired part of my intestinal highway. It provided a safety net for me in case the fragile improvement could not handle the normal flow of traffic. The repair needed time to heal without the labors of movement and digestion, just as I required time to heal without the labors and movement of normal life.

The bag was attached to my abdomen with a sticky gasket and a flat O-ring. It covered a loop of the small intestine and pulled outside the body through a hole cut for that purpose. The intestine—pierced in two places to allow a tube of plastic to pass through it—resembled the handle of a grotesque handbag. Its purpose was to keep the bit of intestine from slithering back into my body where it knew it belonged. To ensure its solid placement, the loop had been secured with stitches around the jagged edge of the inflamed exit. I watched in horror as the bit of protruding intestine danced to its own rhythm of natural peristalsis. I hated the thing even if it was good for me.

From my left side flowed a tube with a plastic grenade-shaped bulb attached to the end. Nurses had clipped it unfashionably to the outside of the johnny. It was filled with a pink liquid the color of strawberry Kool-Aid. But it was not Kool-Aid. The pink hue came from a combination of blood and water. Yes, blood and water flowed from my side. I was reminded of another from whom blood and water had drained. (John 19:34)

I was not alone, not the first.

"Robin, I will heal you." Those words echoed in the caverns of my mind with each unpleasant observation I made.

The details of my ordeal and the possible side-effects of tests and medications—delivered by mouth, nozzle, needle, and medical instruction—were revealed incrementally. I learned to hate surprises. I named this bit-by-bit technique "Disney Line Medicine." I did so in remembrance of the Disneyland lines.

From a distance, the Disney ride lines did not look overwhelming. From the end they looked relatively short. Then, after turning a corner, a new portion of the line was revealed. At the next bend the vista repeated itself. Over and over at each bend, a new length of line was revealed. A deep sense of disappointment accompanied each surprise. If the entire length of the line was visible from the beginning, I would never have stood in it. Disney had the psychological approach to lines thoroughly thought out.

I asked my medical people not to use Disney line psychology on me. I wanted to know what I could be facing from start to finish. No surprises. When I questioned the reasoning of their approach, the doctors told me some patients would be overwhelmed by all the facts. So, I specifically communicated to my caregivers what did and did not work for me. Tiptoeing around facts did *not* work. I realized that their approach was causing me more stress than knowing the facts. There was no way for them to know this unless I said something. They happily accommodated my request, and the stress of any possible "surprise" was eliminated.

As the day progressed, I discovered the anesthesia administered had not only put me out of commission, but it had put my poor intestines to rest as well. Apparently, the intestines take days to awaken. The copious fluids that continued to pump into me began to collect in my belly. I looked "fast-forwardly" pregnant. I began to experience acute pain, so I rang the bell for help. It hurt. I wept. My body, in shock already, had no more room to suffer (so I thought).

Then, the nurse uttered the dreaded abbreviation, "NG tube. You need an NG tube."

"A what?"

"A Nasogastric Tube."

"What does that do?"

"It will be inserted up your nose, down your throat, and into your stomach."

"You're kidding, right?"

I stared at her in disbelief. I was lying in this bed, my body recently torn open and now flooded with fluid. I'd been expanded, stretched, extracted, and my many layers of invaded muscle and flesh had been stitched and continuously drained. Now they wanted to add another revolting ingredient to the mix? Was I being tortured? It couldn't possibly get worse, could it?

It could.

If I wanted relief from this tearing bloat, I was going to have to allow them to put the NG tube in. I felt if I did not allow it, I would explode. The nurse entered with the dreaded tube. She sat me up in the mechanical bed and folded me in half. I felt my wounds cry out in protest. My searing, distended gut folded as well.

"We're going to put this tube up your nose, down your throat and into your stomach, okay?"

"Okay? No, it is not *okay*! Is there any other way?"

"No. Not if you want relief."

I steeled my mind and will to withstand the coming onslaught.

"You may experience gagging."

Really? I gag watching someone gag. I gag imagining that I am going to gag.

"Will I throw up?"

"You might."

"Could I please have something to catch the mess just in case?"

"Sure."

They gave me a large kidney-shaped receptacle. Under my chin it went as the tube went up my nose and down my throat. All this action was accompanied by gagging and choking through tears. Over the teeth, past the gums, look out stomach, here it comes.

And it came.

Success! The tube was in, evidenced by the disgusting, bilious, brown bile that surged upward through it. The up-welling fluid was deposited through a tube into a plastic container that was mounted on the wall behind me like someone's twisted idea of a wall sconce in some haunted house. Weeping, I asked why they hadn't done this while I was still sedated.

"We don't like to do this unless it becomes unavoidable."

I could understand that. But if the intestines tended to become paralyzed for a time after surgery, wouldn't it have been a bit easier to assume it would be needed? I pondered this as my suffering increased. The constant irritation of the tube kept me coughing and adjusting. My throat tried to repel the thing in every way. The only relief came in the form of a tiny numbing cocktail of ice chips and Cepacol. If I didn't move, it did not irritate.

I willed myself not to cough or move. Admittedly, the pain in my gut was immediately relieved. I was to take the bad with the good. I was beginning to learn that there appeared within the shadowy valley an occasional ray of sunshine.

The nurses were efficient and, after the fact, empathetic. They admitted that the NG tube was terrible. They shared with me that the body would try to expel it as long as it was inserted. That's wonderful, I thought. I remained still and immobile to avoid the worst of the irritation.

During the time it took to organize all the bits and pieces of recovery, night had fallen. I looked down and noticed that the bag and the Kool-Aide grenade were filling menacingly fast. I rang the bell for someone, anyone, to come help me. Pain rendered me immobile.

I waited. There was no way to rush the tempo of a hospital. Patience was the order of the day. This was the first of many lessons in this discipline. If I became upset, everything hurt more. So I waited quietly—a prisoner of waste.

An aide finally came to my rescue in the hushed darkness of the hospital night. She appeared to me like an angel draped in human clothing. First she detached me from the wall, then she unplugged Phyllis to free her up for the trip. She lifted my slippers from the floor and placed them gently on my feet one at a time. Then she quietly spoke the words that challenged every fiber of my being, "Okay, can you get up?" She was sincere. And I tried to be too.

"No. I can't lift my feet."

She lifted my feet and moved my legs so they hung over the side of the bed. I could not bend or sit up. She proffered her arm. I grabbed it with both hands and pulled against her anchored frame. We struggled to slide me up to the edge of the bed, my voice and body protesting in unison. I was taken aback by my weakness. My chin slumped on my chest as I tried to imagine how I could gain my footing. We braced again, and she half-lifted me to my feet. The tears rolled down my cheek as I quietly moaned. I hadn't been so dependent on anyone since my years as toddler, and even that I hardly remembered. I was mortified.

We shuffled into the bathroom with Phyllis in tow. The grenade and the bag hung from my side, barely cloaked by the johnny sagging from my shoulders. She lowered me to the seat. I sat there trying to pee with an audience. The nurse—my angel aide—rubbed my back and sang quietly to relax me as I strove to accomplish this simple feat. I was humiliated but too ill to do anything about it. Worse yet, hospital protocol dictated that all fluids in and out were meticulously measured. They made me pee into a measured container hooked to the toilet seat.

Thanks to her kindness and gentle touch, my aide was able to collect her data. I wished to dissolve into the floor and disappear forever. I wept as she held me. Then we took care of the bag and the grenade.

After we had gotten to know one another, she told me that she had been praying for me. I knew it at the time. I could feel it. My beautiful Father was walking with me through the valley. He was at my side. Even in that bathroom, I was not alone.

My angel aide helped me return to bed. The effort to move and accomplish the simplest of tasks exhausted me. My stomach burbled on as it emptied its bloated self into the plastic eyesore attached to the wall. I thought about the pain and humiliation I had experienced in the last twenty-four hours. I never thought it possible that the body could withstand what I had experienced. My spirit cried out, "Father, You said You would heal me. But I am in misery. Where are You in this suffering?"

He responded quietly and firmly to my cries, "I am here in the hands of your surgeons. I am here in the hands of the nurses who come to relieve your pain. I am here with you. These are the hands that I have chosen to help heal you. I am present with them all."

I wondered why He had chosen the long difficult road through the valley. It was too much for me to absorb all His teaching at one time in my weakened, wounded state. He revealed His purpose to me "Disney Line" style as the days and months progressed.

My body cried out for escape. Finally, another dose of relief was delivered through one of Phyllis's tributaries. The medication did its work, and slowly I drifted away.

THE VALLEY

Weakened and wounded, I cast my gaze down the river that wound through the valley. Wet stone walls loomed above me. Along their ramparts jutted great slabs of rock whose shadows hid unknown mysteries. A light mist fell from the sky. In the background, behind the rush of water, I thought I could hear strange rustling and tapping. I listened, my ears like a fox, focused with laser precision. What could be making these noises? Nothing was visible in the gray light.

My pack carried much of what I would need to survive this journey. Still, I would have to move forward if I wished to live. I reached above my head for another rock to grasp. They were scattered everywhere, having fallen in past storms from their precarious perches. I pulled and dragged myself a few inches farther from the edge of the river. The pack was slowly becoming dislodged with each slippery effort. My legs dragged uselessly.

I finally gained some ground and put the river a safe distance beneath me. I lay miserable and wet in the mud. I couldn't move while dragging my muddied anchor, so I detached some of the many buckles on my pack. After a while, I ceased struggling and surrendered to my exhaustion. Sleep came immediately.

Unintelligible whispering echoed and blended with the rush of water. It surrounded me from everywhere and nowhere simultaneously. Large and small shadows circled slowly above my head. A whoosh of dark wings passed close by, and a quiet raspy voice snarled in my ear. "You will never leave this place." Another circle. "You will die here on the banks of this forsaken river." The wings departed, trailing a dank smell in its wake. My nose recoiled in disgust. I thought I felt something drag across my face.

Night had settled around me. I floated on the precipice of sleep. Strange dreams plagued my unconscious mind. I thought I saw creatures hiding in the walls above me. There were great birds of many sizes perched with dark, folded wings. They whispered and stared with beady eyes from their stony turrets.

Suddenly there was light. I woke cold and stiff. My panting breath formed light clouds in the dampness. Where was I? Oh yes, I was way down here. My foggy thoughts began to focus, and I remembered falling. I remembered the tumbling punishing water. I was stuck. I wondered how I was ever going to get out of this place.

I experimented in an effort to turn onto my side. My stomach was wounded—but dragging my body backward through the mud was not going to move me down the river. At least the rain was letting up. I reached across my body with my right hand and pulled. Accompanied by loud groaning and stabbing pain, I succeeded. I began to worm downriver on my side. From above, I must have looked like a confused inchworm. I didn't care. I was moving.

I studied the wall opposite the river. As the rain cleared, more detail became visible. The walls across the river rose just as steeply as those looming above me. Climbing directly out of the valley was out of the question. I inched forward and listened.

The river roared and echoed and whispered. Every fiber of my body tightened, like a violin string waiting to be plucked. As I inched forward, a great shadow passed above me. In my awkward position, I could not look upward to see what had caused it. Whatever it was had been quite large. I continued to fight for ground with my ears hyperaware—like prey.

❁

PAIN

I awoke in the middle of the night. Pain assaulted me. I had never experienced this kind of torture. Like a predator on the hunt, my pain charged my door, threw its shoulder against the lock, and barged in. I fled backward and cowered against the far wall of my entryway. It crowded in after me. Undeterred, it pressed its powerful bulk forward and placed its forearm on my neck. It slammed me back against the wall and held me immobile at knife point. I froze in shock, my voice choked to a stillness in my throat.

I never wanted to become acquainted with this beast. But here it was in its enormous bulk, an invader of my space, my safety. Here it loomed and threatened, poised to kill me.

I rang for the nurse. The beast lurked and stabbed. She came. I could barely speak, but my eyes told her the story.

"Are you in pain?" she whispered. It was night. The atmosphere in the hospital resonated *sotto voce*.

I could only nod and stare.

"We'll get you something for that."

Minutes later she arrived with the solution and injected it into one of the tubes flowing from Phyllis' branches. I waited for it to take effect. A moment later, the forearm of the beast withdrew from my neck. I drew a deep breath. The beast's knife slowly withdrew from my belly. I had not died as I thought I would. I had survived. The invading monster skulked out the door to pace the hallway. It's clicking claws tapped a constant reminder of its waiting presence.

Pain medication ushered much-needed sleep over the threshold and into my room. I slid slowly down, and the dark walls of the canyon engulfed me once again.

❀

INTRODUCTION TO WARFARE

P ain became a bigger obstacle as I dragged myself along the riverbank. I thought about the uncharted distance I might have to travel and became overwhelmed. I would have to think in inches and feet. Reach. Grab. Pull. Never give up. Never give up. Move forward inch by inch.

My job was to stay alive and escape from this valley.

Progress was slow. I wormed through an alien environment, vulnerable to the unknown. Fear prowled the edges of my thoughts. I was tired—immeasurably tired—but I pressed on to avoid sleep. I had no idea what I might encounter lurking in the dark recesses of my mind. But despite my valiant effort to outrun sleep, it spread its wings over me and I settled into a world of shadows.

"Who are you kidding? You'll never get out of here," came the whisper. Something circled above me, its dark wings extended. It brushed my face with dangling talons. It laughed and cackled, mocking me, "How are you going to climb these walls? You can barely move. See how I can fly? I can adjust my wings and be out of the valley within seconds. But you—you will be here forever."

I awoke in another fit of panic. Still, I struggled onward. Reach, grab, pull, never give up. I dragged myself forward.

I had to focus and visualize my way out. I could not listen to the whispering voice that circled above. But the pain was relentless. It swooped down like a bird of prey and sank its talons into my side. Blood flowed down onto the bank and diluted the water pink.

As I wormed my way down the canyon, my eyes cast their gaze high above me on the craggy walls. Vigilant, I searched the dark shadows above for what might emerge. I was overcome with a heavy foreboding.

I looked to my left and felt a tearing stab of pain on my right side. I turned to face the source of the pain and felt another stabbing on my left. The bird had moved from my dreams into the daylight, and it had brought more of its kind along to help. Cleverly, they hunted for an opening to attack.

I became distressed—more vulnerable to the bites and tears from beaks and talons. As thoughts of doom invaded my mind, the large creature who had assaulted me in my dream materialized overhead. Its huge wings overshadowed me; its dangling talons were draped with putrid flesh. I heard the horrible croaking voice and smelled its dank, moldy breath as it cackled and laughed. "Yes, fear. You will suffer and die here. No one knows where you are."

I had two choices: succumb to fear and self-pity, and die here, or fight to save my life. I chose to fight.

"No, I will not be here forever. I will get out." I shouted at the putrid creature. I had a feeling it could hear my thoughts, but I yelled anyway. Flinging my declaration like a weapon provided me strength.

I dragged myself forward as the birds intensified their assault. They stabbed and bit every space my flailing arms could not protect. Bit by bit, inch by squirming inch, I pushed forward.

As I persisted, the birds lessened their assaults. They still attacked, but their beaks and claws did not pierce my flesh as deeply. As I kept moving, the pain of their blows began to diminish. It was great motivation to continue.

Suddenly there was movement behind me. I stopped cold, slowly casting my gaze over my shoulder. Something else was following me. Two shimmering shapes floated behind me in the gloom. They hovered just above the ground and faded in and out of focus as I lay frozen in place. They were fluid, luminous. They caught my eye but kept their distance as I stared.

A barely audible sound began to emanate from within and around them. It was music unlike anything I'd heard before. It resonated gently, and the air seemed to oscillate around and between these figures. As I listened, I heard the resonating hum of a harmonic series. Subtle but unmistakable—the stack of intervals built to a crescendo until the rocks in the walls began to vibrate.

As the rocks vibrated, they sang a series of intervals that harmonized with those of the beings. The water soon entered with its own song. The sounds all blended with the stones and the creatures into a symphony of physics and harmony. Each shining mineral and each sparkle of light sang its own song. As I listened, the world where I lay began to fade away. I rested, my eyes fastened upon the glowing beings, and let the sound and beauty enfold me like a warm, weightless comforter.

Suddenly, the screech of the birds shattered the music. The symphony disappeared, and the ephemeral creatures vaporized into the mist.

✵

WARFARE

I awoke in the early hours of the morning and lay on my bed in misery. Self-pity and mistrust lurked on the perimeter of my mind. Because God had spoken His promise to heal me, it became my responsibility to believe. Faith and gratitude became my two most effective weapons in the war against fear.

Be faithful. That was my first command. I had asked God in the past what I could do for Him. His response to me each time had been, "Trust Me." He had spoken His promise to heal me. I did not see it at the moment, but I needed to hold my shield of faith, to believe without seeing (Eph. 6:16). I had heard His whisper as I passed through the waters. It was a familiar and quiet utterance. I had heard it before and seen miraculous results. I knew He never lied.

"Robin, I will heal you."

That quiet promise became my war cry. The internal dialogue raged on.

"You are lying here in this bed in misery."

Negative thoughts took a third-person form and spoke to me from outside my body.

"Where is your God now?" the voice sneered mockingly. "He said He would heal you. Why do you have to go through this? He could touch you in an instant and it would be done."

"Trust Me," the quiet voice whispered.

I imagined myself as a soldier in battle. I thought of David and his fight with Goliath the Philistine giant (I Sam. 17.). David was the youngest of Jesse's eight sons. In the eyes of his family, David was just a little shepherd boy who nobody thought much of. But he was the one who possessed the courage to take on a tenacious, tireless, arrogant enemy.

This little shepherd boy killed a nine-foot giant with one fling of a stone. The stone flew powered by a slingshot, but hit its mark powered by faith. He'd had no fear, only trust.

"You said you would heal me." I spoke to God in my thoughts.

The promise bounced back and forth in my mind like an echoing river between walls of a narrow canyon. This was a foothold—a handhold I could use to pull myself forward toward recovery.

This war cry was not a one-time declaration. My enemy was persistent. "You are lying here in pain. You can't even get out of bed to use the bathroom. Your gut is wounded. Your very core has been sliced open, and more than a pound of your flesh was extracted. Bits of your insides are hanging out of your body. It is ugly. Disgusting. You are in misery. This could go on forever."

I spoke to myself in the third person as well. I had to demand more from my inner soldier. "Be grateful Robin." That second command echoed within the valleys of my mind. I was tough on myself. I became my own drill instructor. I felt as if I had entered a demanding and meticulous training of the mind. I was reminded of the military training the elite teams in our armed services go through. Their training goes beyond the physical. The mind, will, and determination are honed. I knew that the military mindset had saved lives. I was a soldier in the army of God. Now my elite training was in session.

I had to fight. I asked—we do not have because we do not ask (James 4:2)—that God's strength be with me, that He would fight this battle for and with me. And so, the battle raged on.

I commanded myself, "Stop it, you baby. Be grateful for what you have. There are people in the world in much worse shape than you. Think of veterans who have been wounded in battle! They've been shot and tortured. They were not resting in comfortable hospital beds with nurses close by to answer their every call. They did not have pain medication delivered to them whenever it was needed. They did not have aides to help them move. They may have been dragged by medics over rocky terrain. There were no showers, no blankets, no comforts. They were lying in blood, dirt, and weather while their enemy rained death upon them. How dare you complain. Be grateful for the blessings you've been provided."

Be grateful. It was a command, not a suggestion. As my helplessness assaulted me, gratitude for my caregivers increased. I was able to make them smile and laugh, which became a medicine of its own for me. Each time I succeeded in making someone happy, I noticed my pain and stress diminish. It became my challenge to make these busy, helpful angels happy and relaxed in my presence. After a few days, they began to tell me how much they enjoyed coming into my room. Kindness had become a joy and an effective pain reliever.

I also drew strength as I thought about children in hospitals all around the world. Innocent children and their parents were experiencing far worse suffering than I. Gratitude became a weapon of ever-increasing effectiveness. The more I used it, the better it performed. It became a deadly sniper targeting the thoughts sneaking in to attack my emotional and spiritual equilibrium.

As time progressed, I found that the mental discipline of recovery was as important—if not more important—than the physical challenges I had to overcome. A joyful heart and a mind infused with gratitude and hope produced in me the energy I needed to heal. I was provided a light in the dark tunnel of illness. And that light shone as I moved through the valley of shadows.

WARRIORS

The cries of the birds had shattered my reverie. My heart pounded in my chest. I gasped for air to fill my aching lungs. I forced myself to move forward. Quaking fearfully in place was not going to improve my chances of escape from this valley.

Time passed, my breathing slowed, and my heart settled into a less frantic rhythm. Perhaps I had imagined that entire episode? But the rock walls rose high above me, and the shadows that cast from great protruding boulders quickened my dark imagination.

I squirmed forward. Slowly the river began to widen and settle. As I made my way around the first bend, the sky began to clear. Watery rays of sunlight found their way into the canyon. A sigh of relief escaped my lips and a faint smile flickered over my face.

There were fewer rocks here. The rough terrain had been smoothed by the slow, regular flow of the river over the years. Here grasses had responded to the increased light and a soft carpet of green spread itself out in front of me. I inched forward onto it. A wave of relief washed over me, and a deep groan cascaded from my lips. I released my pack one buckle at a time and rolled—or more accurately, flopped—onto my back. The soft grass afforded great relief from the scraping, pebbly mud. I lay motionless on the ground.

I rested in the warm light. The grass held me like a mother holds a child. Gentle sun washed over my face and blanketed me in warmth while nearby a soft stream of water sang a lullaby and put me to sleep.

I dreamed.

Above me, high atop the jagged stone parapets that loomed over the valley, banks of clouds began to materialize. They formed slowly at first. Then, as the heat of the day sent streams of air rising, they burst upward with power and expanded into immense explosive creations. As I watched, there formed within the billows—faintly at first—the shapes of great chariots. They slowly burgeoned upward from the bank.

As I continued to stare, the shapes of horses' heads manifested themselves. Behind them, bodies materialized. The horses leaned forward, harnessed in strong golden light in front of the chariots. I stared wide-eyed at the drama that played above me. Horses and chariots were lined along the entire perimeter of my constricted view. They surrounded the valley with a mighty presence. It was both staggering and terrifying. I had never seen anything like it. Perhaps my injuries had affected my eyesight? It must be my imagination, I thought. There are no chariots in the sky.

As I watched, the horses began to pull the chariots forward. They reared, neighed, and beat the air with their front hooves. The sound rolled like thunder.

Upon the chariots there appeared riders. They were equipped for battle. Arrayed in armor, they carried weapons—magnificent swords and shields. Their feet were shod with sandals. Wings covered their bodies; their heads, shielded with helmets, glowed with blinding light.

The clouds began to luminescence with fiery red light. The entire sky above them was illuminated with all the colors of the rainbow diffused throughout the sky (Ez. 1: 22). I heard the warriors crying out with voices that rushed like great waters. They spoke a language unknown to me, but it seemed that the heavens understood and responded with an undulating light show.

I awoke amazed. The sights and feelings of my dream lingered with me. I lay there warm and still, strangely at peace.

But considering my circumstances, how could I be at peace? Nevertheless, peace surrounded me and filled me with effervescent joy. This was certainly a fearful and wonderful place into which I had fallen. The soft grass and the warm honey sun high above me offered a welcome respite from the muddy, painful struggle of the past days.

But it was time to move. I was tempted by the thought of staying and resting under those glorious horses and chariots, but time was something I could not afford to waste.

Even so, in my dream-like state, I ignored time's insistent pull and remained silent and still, held by the grass in the warmth of the sun.

❁

Time

There was form and rhythm in the hospital. In the morning, the march commenced. Everyone marched in, performed their respective tasks, then marched out. At six a.m., the parade began:

March

Time for the blood test.
Time for the blood clot shot.
Time to check the fluids in.
Time to check the fluids out.
Time for nurse to check the meds.
Time to clean the messy beds.
Time for maids to clean the room.
Time! The doctor's coming soon.
Get up, get clean, then walk around.
Go back to bed.
Begin again.

The morning progressed, and the flurry of activity eased as the first press dissolved into their daily tasks. Gradually the tempo and rhythm of the day slowed. Time stretched out before me like a long pedal point beneath changing harmony.

There was grace in illness. I was too sick to care. I settled into a gently rocking set of threes. Aided by pain medication and accompanied by cooking shows, my eyes devoured what my body could not. I was not yet able to expand my palate beyond gourmet chips and sips. I watched people cook and eat, and I wafted through the day. I floated as imaginary aromas and tastes surrounded my suffering body. The simple pleasures became all there were. I could do nothing about it.

There was a certain freedom in my lack of control. The key to peace was to accept the fact that I could do nothing to change my circumstances. When my thoughts invaded, I drew my weapon of gratitude and my shield of faith. The voice that echoed through my mind repeated, "Robin, I will heal you," over and over. Thoughts of the soldiers, whom I prayed for regularly, passed through my mind. Their plight dwarfed mine. "Robin," I commanded myself, "stop whining. Enjoy the imaginary pizza."

Time lacked measured bars. Instead, it flowed like Gregorian chant—melody and flexible rhythm that ebbs, floods, and floats through space. The staff operated like a regiment of soldiers, but my space was set apart, private, defined by a closed door that shut the hospital's chaos away.

The world was shut away as well. I was enclosed behind walls and doors like a monk. Time beyond those walls had nothing to do with our processes. Time was suspended, and this was a place for healing. We could not work, do chores, or take care of others. We healed. That was our job. I read my tiny to-do list. The nurses listed my little tasks on a diminutive white board hung on the wall. It typically consisted of no more than a few short lines: wake up, get up, clean up, walk. That was it. It was wonderful.

When evening arrived, the lights were dimmed and the tempo in the hospital slowed to an adagio. Dynamics were hushed. Nurses and aides floated quietly in and out, tending to their wounded patients like suspended harmonies barely touching the floor. Everything happened quietly and in slow-motion. The only exception was my intravenous friend, Phyllis. She was the only being who ignored protocol. She yelled and screamed whenever she needed anything—regardless of time or her patient's desire for blessed unconsciousness.

THE CHARIOTEER

I bobbed and rocked as if resting upon the water. The dreams and experiences from the last couple days swam lazily to the surface of my thoughts. They spun themselves out—slow-motion pictures displayed on the screen of my memory. I reviewed them carefully, digesting each in turn. I had experienced malevolent evil counterbalanced with overwhelming good. I felt as if there was an immense battle raging somewhere. A battle I could not quite see.

Warmth permeated my body. The sunlight reflected off the water and glistened upward along the walls of the canyon. The dancing reflections beckoned me onward. I enjoyed the show for a few minutes, but my stomach demanded attention. I knew I had a long haul, or crawl, ahead of me. I needed to feed myself to continue.

My tumble through the air and water, through bouts of panic and sheer terror, had distracted me until now. I remembered that I had brought food, but I had to access my pack to get it. Sleep and time supine, combined to stiffen every muscle in my body. I slowly reached to unfasten the pack from my arm. My every motion became a monument to the events of the past few days. I had never felt pain like this.

A hoarse whisper echoed against the stone: "You will never get out of here." My head snapped up. Where had that voice come from? It was familiar. It was the voice from my dream. Was that thing here now? I looked behind me but could see nothing.

"I heard you," I said to nothing, "and I will not listen. I will get out of here."

I reached for the contents in my pack. I had prepared carefully. To reach the food, I had to manipulate zippers and the internal stay-dry packages that protected it. The food was simple: protein bars, nuts, and fruit. I had not planned to hike for days. I had to ration.

I allowed myself half a protein bar and washed it down with water from the camel in my pack. Slowly, shimmers of life began to radiate throughout my body. It was time to move on. I had to leave this grassy harbor and continue my fight to survive.

I slipped the pack straps up onto my shoulders and hitched it around my hips. By act of sheer will, I dragged my body forward from one small goal to the next.

The terrain remained tame for a short while. I was not able to see much beyond where I'd struggled due to the curvature of the canyon and the steep walls. I kept my eyes trained on the stones that loomed above me. The brief sunlight had spent its time down here. But now slowly it crept up the slippery walls toward the top. I wished I could float and follow it to escape the darkness.

I dragged myself onward, refusing to allow fear to perch my mind. I knew the monster circled above me somewhere. Wind stirred from its wings and brushed lightly over my neck, sending goosebumps slithering down my back and arms.

As the day began to fade, I searched for a safe place to bed for the night. This valley was cold and damp, so I needed to keep as warm and dry as possible. I wished I knew the flora and fauna better. I needed relief from the pain and imagined there were herbs or plants that could serve that purpose. Oh, how lovely it would be if I was numb. Oblivion beckoned to me.

I slid toward the walls blocking my progress and tucked myself beneath one of the protruding rock ledges in case it rained during the night. I pulled the wrap from my pack and settled onto the hard, damp ground.

Exhaustion overwhelmed the pain in a great wave of unconsciousness.

Then they came—dark-winged beasts and their sharp beaks. They pierced my flesh with their talons. They had settled on me for their meal. Others circled above, seeking space to land. Burning pain seared me from chest to toe. My face contorted as I gazed upward to look for relief. I tried to cry out for help, but my voice caught in my throat. No sound escaped my panic-stricken lips.

From the corner of my eye, I thought I could see the charioteers on the ramparts. I stared, frozen in place. One turned his head in my direction. His compelling gaze met mine. His eyes, those of a warrior, glowed with passion and red-hot fire.

As the beasts surrounded me and administered their punishment, I saw him lift his arm to signal his great horse. The chariot turned in my direction and began to move. As it did, it reflected the luminous glow from the sky and illuminated the flock of tormentors surrounding me.

I marveled at the sight. The birds circled and dove, tearing bits of my flesh each time they touched me. My arms flailed uselessly as I tried to fend them off. I batted at them and raised my hands to guard my face.

Suddenly, movement caught my eye. The horse and chariot manned by the glowing warrior lifted from the ramparts and descended into the valley. Billows of roiling cloud followed in their wake.

There was a sound like rushing wind, and the tumbling clouds expanded behind them. They were coming straight for me. Light from the heavens began to infiltrate the canyon.

I was a tiny being crouched in the darkness, surrounded by screeching, circling birds of prey. I watched with wonder as the warrior approached. I could hear him speaking to the creatures above me. I could not understand the language, but I could sense the power behind it. As the horse and chariot neared, the creatures began to lose their interest in me. They veered their yellow gazes upward.

The golden glow of the charioteer illuminated the entire scene. The birds beat against air with furious wings. They screamed, clawed, and tore at one another—thankfully missing my flesh in the process. I realized they were panicking. They're lives were suddenly threatened between the canyon walls.

They turned in the air and aimed their talons skyward, but to no avail. The flock of tormentors became the tormented. I gazed upward, transfixed by the sight. The besieged flock was suddenly confused. They attacked one another and scattered explosively. Then, in an instant, above me there remained only empty space and silence between the darkening canyon walls.

Coaching

Morning arrived. In marched the parade. Out marched the parade. The to-do list was becoming habit. The white board let the nurses know I needed assistance. I was not yet independent. I needed to be unhooked from the wall and helped with the dreaded bag. But today there would be new and exciting developments.

My nurse arrived, and I inquired about the trophy on the wall. It seemed my stomach had stopped distending and my bilious wall hanging was not filling at its normal pace. She asked, matter-of-factly, "How is your stomach feeling? Are you farting yet?" Her questions were shocking. In normal conversation outside these walls, it would have been unthinkable. And yet she repeated, "Are you farting yet?"

"Uh ... Yes, I think so."

"Are they wet or dry?"

I looked at her quizzically. Nurses said the darndest things. "Uh, dry?"

"Are you in pain? Does your belly hurt here?"

She pressed my formerly distended abdomen and let it bounce happily back. Everything within my newly repaired intestine and muscular wall shook. "Hmm, seems to be better," she smiled. "I think we can take the NG tube out. Are you ready for that?"

"Oh, yes ma'am! Will it hurt or make me throw up like it did on the way in?"

"Oh no," she said. "It's easy."

I did not believe a word. She left the room and came back in with equipment. "Okay, ready?" she said.

"Sure, I'm ready." I drew in a deep breath, one that would make any professional flutist proud, and as she pulled, I assisted. I blew that thing out using my highly developed diaphragmatic power. I blew it out of her hands and halfway down my belly. I think I shocked the poor woman.

"Why did you blow out like that?" She wanted to know, I think, because she had been sprayed by the accompanying shower power. "There was no need for that! The tube comes out easily!"

"I didn't believe you. I was just trying to help."

She wiped off her ungloved hands and everything else that had been in range. She was not pleased, but I was. I smiled surreptitiously. The scratching, invasive intruder was gone. I was free! No more need for Cepacol and ice to dim the 24/7 burn of the NG. I was detached from one thing at least, though the nurse forgot to take down the bag from the wall. It hung there like a spiderweb-covered memento from another century—a bilious tribute to suffering.

The next day she came in and apologized. She told me she had been awake during the night worrying about how she'd left the bag there. It really was a loathsome reminder, but I was moved that it had bothered her so.

That was not the only new break in routine for the morning. A beautiful young nurse with flowing hair and a benevolent demeanor soared in and announced, smiling, that she was a specialist. She was the expert on the ileostomy bag, and she was here to answer any questions I had. Oh, goody!

"So, have you been emptying your own bag? How's it going?"

"No, I haven't been."

"Why not?" She gazed pointedly at me from beneath her well-groomed brows. "You should be doing that now."

"It's repulsive. I don't want to touch that thing." I hadn't been able to bring myself to do it. I was still in shock.

But she forced me to do it. Smiling, she walked me into the bathroom and stood there watching as I emptied the putrid bag attached to my stomach. I insisted upon using gloves.

I know she forced me for my own good. Eventually I was going to have to do this at home, but I did not want to start yet.

After the voidance of the exit ramp, she proceeded to teach me about the importance of proper bag closure. She gave me a few options to try, then set me up with detailed instructions for each method. Failure to complete this important task correctly could lead to disastrous results.

I felt like a helpless child. Never had I experienced so much humiliation in such a short time. I wanted to disappear. But there was no way to escape her persistent, pleasant presence.

We returned to the room, and she began to discuss the finer points of dealing with the bag. The main challenge was to keep the bag comfortably on the abdomen while preventing leakage. It sounded simple. She went on to explain the types of adhesive closures, disks, O-rings, and covers that were available. There were different styles and sizes of bags as well. And, she shared, there also existed lingerie to conceal the intruder—just in case this process lasted a lifetime.

We then focused on detailed steps for bag replacement and closure, both of which were extremely important. These particulars were driven home by trial and error after my return from the hospital. Managing the bag proved to be a long, strenuous learning process—one I never quite mastered.

She hooked me up with a company that would deliver the equipment to my home and left me piles of literature. She told me that the equipment would come accompanied by a nurse who specialized in the process until I became comfortable doing it myself. I never became comfortable with all of it, and I took solace knowing I would not be completely alone during the process. I was slightly relieved for the time being. Little did I know what was in store for me upon my arrival home.

As my stay in hospital continued, I'd been made responsible for one more task: changing my own bag. The diminutive white board reflected the change to my nurses and aides. I was becoming independent. Slowly but surely, the healing process was beginning.

I counted my simple blessings: I could get out of bed without assistance; I could clean myself independently; I walked and danced with Phyllis on a daily basis; and—what a delight—I could take care of my bathroom needs without an audience. There was always something for which to be grateful.

❀

LITTLE NURSE LITTLE STEPS

Another day dawned. The routine repeated itself again at 6:00 a.m.: blood tests, blood clot shot, vitals, IV bag change, medications administered. During these ministrations, I noticed the bulb— my Kool-Aid grenade—was not as full as it had been on previous days. I mentioned this to my nurse. She agreed. It was time to remove the drain.

Later that morning, a fresh-faced little thing pranced into the room. From my perspective, she looked to be about fourteen—no doubt a rookie. "Hello," she piped pleasantly. "Let's get this drain out of you."

"Will it hurt?" Simple question, I thought.

"Um, I don't know."

"You don't know?"

With that response, I figured I was headed for trouble. This little girl did not know what she was doing. Nevertheless, she bent her head to focus on the task at hand. I prepared to become a part of her learning process.

She began to pull the tube. I felt something interesting deep inside me. I had no idea where the end of this drain was situated. She pulled again, and I gasped and grabbed her arm for support. She probably should have put a piece of leather or a stick in my mouth for me to bite down on. I may have hurt her, I'm not certain, because she hopped back and immediately scampered for help.

The next minute a real nurse appeared. Like an angel, she proffered her arm and I grabbed tightly with both hands. The little girl proceeded to pull again. I gasped. I'd never even imagined pain like this. Nor had I realized these parts of my body existed. I had no doubt they were there now. I cried out like a woman in travail.

Little nurse continued to pull. Slowly, the bloody length of tube increased in her hands. It was long. Where had this drain been resting these last few days?

Finally, after much arm squeezing and groaning, the drain reached the end of its tunnel and rested just beneath my skin. "One last pull," she said. She smiled, and the drain was delivered.

I marveled at its appearance. It was long and rectangular in shape. It was covered with tiny holes that had absorbed the blood and water collecting inside my wounds. I was shocked at the shape. It was a square peg in a round space and had not lent itself to smooth extraction, though I figured the rectangle afforded more surface area for drainage. I wondered, could it not have been designed in a more ergonomic manner?

I spoke to the child, and because she had asked me to describe how the removal felt, I told her to share with her future patients that it felt like giving birth backwards. I smiled as she departed.

I smiled as well, for there now hung upon me one less vestige of my surgery. A simple gauze bandage marked the spot where the offending bulb had hung. My grenade was no more. One less trophy displaying the residuals of my ordeal. I was thrilled. Another step toward recovery had been taken.

It was time to walk. Time to take Phyllis for her stroll. So, lighter one grenade, I set out for my daily shuffle. Phyllis and I traveled out into the hall to challenge the speed and distance of yesterday's training. I must have been feeling a bit better, for I suddenly noticed the people and activities that surrounded us.

The first thing my competitive instinct observed was that I was, by far, the slowest moving person in sight. Other patients could *walk*, whereas I inched along. They were motoring along at almost a normal speed. Staff moved like Olympians. What was wrong with me? Even though I held Phyllis as a support, I could barely manage to lift my feet off the floor.

Because I moved in slow-motion, I had time to notice the visual details of those passing me in their daily promenade. I made a list of hospital fashion choices in my mind as I moved through the hallway. We were uniformed, wounded warriors united by our fashion. We all looked like we had hired the same demented designer.

The most noticeable pieces were hospital johnnies. The johnny was constructed in a way that gave doctors, nurses, and aides access to whatever parts of the body they needed to access. There were snaps and ties in the most unusual places. Trying to don an unsnapped johnny was a task that required concentration and know-how. My arm would always end up somewhere it was not supposed to be.

The ties were in two strategic places. One was behind the neck and the other—the most important—was somewhere behind. That one was the most difficult to find but also the one most essential to complete closure. Some of my fellow patients were less diligent in their efforts to ensure proper implementation of this feature. One such gentleman preceded me in my walk the day of my drain removal. As he quick-stepped in front of me, the breeze perilously billowed his garment. He moved forward with strides dangerously long for someone robed in partially-secured vestments.

There were others who chose alternative strategies, one of which I named the twofer. This person wore two johnnies in place of one. The first was worn as intended, while the other was used as safety net of sorts—worn backwards with the closures to the front. This strategy provided extra security and warmth. Considering the less-than-moderate temperatures in the hallways, I thought it a smart idea.

The second major fashion statement was modeled by another man making his rounds. I dubbed this "the drawstring pant"— light as air, no pressure anywhere. I adopted the style for myself as the days passed, though the inseam was constructed for people tall enough to play in the NBA.

The hospital also offered lightweight disposable boxer shorts—perfect for any patients seeking a painless, zero-maintenance solution to coverage.

Accent pieces were available in the form of nonskid slipper-socks. There were two choices of color: mustard yellow and mint green. Most of the men sported the yucky yellow. I chose the cool mint to compliment my tube sock IV protector and the ever-present rubber band I donned on my wrist. The hospital fashion and remnants of clothing from home that comprised the collection were displayed in a slow-motion elliptical runway show.

We negotiated daily the obligatory promenade around the track-like floor encircling the central offices. Differing speeds, differing motivations, and differing fashions circled the area that they—our caregivers—said would lead to a speedier recovery and our eventual escape.

We pressed toward the mark. We fought to finish our race. We were a remnant of soldiers united by our struggle for healing and our battle-worn uniforms of pain and suffering.

FOOD AND FEAR

I'd been on a liquid diet for weeks. But not the fun kind consisting of smoothies and juices. This one was designed to keep me alive. It offered no enjoyment, no flavor. I watched cooking shows to satisfy that need.

But the white board reflected a change. Chips and sips were augmented with clear broths! I was still not allowed to chew. They gave me a menu. It was labeled "post-surgery" On it were printed, in true restaurant style, all my options. It looked almost like a real menu, but only one that would satisfy those unwell enough to disdain the thought of food.

I perused my options: black coffee, black tea, chicken bouillon, beef bouillon, Jell-O, lemon, lime, or raspberry sherbet—depending upon the day—and, oh joy, vegetable soup puree. I asked my nurse what her recommendation might be. She steered me away from the bullion and toward the vegetable soup instead. I do not like vegetables, so I was skeptical. Perhaps pureed, they might be palatable. I took the risk and phoned down to the cafeteria. This hospital had room service. A patient could order food whenever they wished, and it would be delivered forty-five minutes later. I had never seen anything like it in any other hospital I had visited.

For nearly a month everything I had eaten had produced pain. It was easy not to eat when every bite delivered a variation on the theme of torture. Food was on its way for the first time in a long time—but for the first time in my life, I was afraid to eat.

Exactly forty-five minutes after my call, a person dressed in formal black and white attire arrived at my door and politely knocked.

"Foodzzhere. Where do ya wan' me ta put it?"

"Right here on my handy dandy adjustable table, thanks."

The tray was placed strategically. I stared at my banquet, unmoved. It included: black tea, vegetable soup, and lemon ice. I lifted the heat retention lid and dipped my spoon tentatively. I was afraid. Was this going to tear through me? And what was going to happen inside on my newly constructed exit ramp?

I had never had to worry about an exit ramp before. Everyone I asked—and I asked over and over for certainty—told me to try a little bit at a time and wait and see. So, I tried. I waited. I saw. Twenty minutes later I saw exactly what happened in the small intestine on the way down. Just as planned, the exit ramp worked. I had never been down this road before, and neither had my food. The only pain I felt (besides the pain from surgery, which already besieged me) was the need to empty the cursed bag more often. In my mind, it became reason enough to starve myself. At least the lemon ice had its rewards. It felt good going down and tasted much better than the imaginary food I had been consuming.

Everything was new both inside and out: new plumbing, new scars, new gear, and a new body. I was going to have to get used to a lot of "new" in the coming months. Also new was the lack of trust I had in my body. For the first time, it had let me down.

I was surprised by how betrayed I felt. I responded to my recent developments the way a puppy responds to new sounds. Their little head tilts back and forth and their eyes reflect a quizzical gaze. I stared with a furrowed brow and tilted head at my alien stomach with the same lack of understanding and disbelief. I'd never had a reason to expect the worst when it came to my health. I considered myself fortunate to have had this much time to enjoy good health before my core decided to rebel. I had taken many things for granted over the years—including the inner workings of my digestive tract.

The bag did its job. It was part of the process that had just saved my life. But it was also a poor substitute for the original. It did not perform as efficiently as the former model. I missed my large intestine. I had never imagined I would have cause to miss my large intestine. Now I appreciated it more than ever before. It taught me a life lesson: never take for granted even the simplest or most basic asset. One never knows if or when it will be snatched away. Always be grateful, even for the littlest things.

I was struck by the miraculous construction of my body. Something as basic as a sphincter muscle—our body's version of an O-ring—could make such a tremendous difference in a person's quality of life. I thought about the difference the O-ring on the space shuttle Challenger had made in so many lives. Without it, a space craft might never have escaped the bounds of earth. But when it malfunctioned, it took and altered countless lives. Gratitude was fundamental.

I'd made tiny steps of progress. I was no longer attached to as many things as I had been in previous days. The operating room IV nurse removed the specialized large-bore IV they had left in "just in case" I had to return to the operating room. That possibility had been hanging over my head for a couple of days.

I had no more grenade and no more trophy bag of bile. I learned to be grateful for the little things. Now I had taken my first step towards real food. It was a beginning.

As the days progressed, my surgeon intermittently popped in with his team to monitor my progress. He liked to move things along. Since everything seemed to be going well, I was graduated from the sparse post-operative menu to the next rung on the healing ladder. I could have toast, chicken, and pasta! I was able to eat food that needed chewing (and they made sure I knew to chew properly). "Chew completely," they said. "Make sure of it." I should have been deliriously happy—but the fear lingered. Each new step provoked mystery. What would happen when I ate something new? It became a waiting game: try, wait, imagine the worst, hope for the best.

With my introduction to new foods came more education regarding the function of my exit ramp. A nurse talked to me about what would work with my gear and what would not. I received paperwork and lists. There were foods recommended and foods forbidden. Disobeying instructions could result in the clogging of the exit and the shutting down of all traffic through it, which could result in another surgery. Meticulous behavior on my part was essential.

Everything that entered my mouth exited through my new construction. I was able to see exactly what the small intestine had been doing all these years. I was amazed to learn that the speed of flow through that mysterious tunnel could be controlled by the types of foods eaten. I was able to see exactly how one food differed from another. If not for the pain and disgust involved, it would've made for a fascinating educational experience.

Medical personnel continued to measure everything that went in and out of me. Apparently, it was extremely important that things not flow too quickly so I would not become dehydrated. Certain foods increased speed of flow and certain foods slowed them down. I had no idea my diet could double as an accelerator or brake.

I also had no idea that most of the water and fluid we consume gets absorbed within the large intestine. The small intestine partially digests food. The large intestine finishes the job and reabsorbs the water. To avoid the complications of dehydration, I was instructed to drink more fluids than usual. That translated to an increased workload for my drill instructor bladder. It forced me to continue my fitness training. I was up and down like a gymnast on a trampoline—but with far less grace.

The point is, I was moving. I was getting up and down with far more ease and regularity. I remembered how I had felt just a few days earlier, and my sense of gratitude swelled. I was improving. A gentle ray of hope had dawned in my heart. There was an end in sight. But would it prove to just be a "Disney Line" end?

CRUTCHES

The sun splashed upon my face and woke me. I must have slept late into the morning for the sun to be so far overhead. My heart pounded, my breathing came fast and labored. The images from my dream played out again in my mind: cloud warriors and birds of prey at war. I teetered between the world of dreams and the stark world of reality, not quite sure which I had just entered. Slowly, reality refocused itself before me. My struggle forward had to begin. So I dislodged myself from my spot and began again to inch forward.

As I moved, I planned for what could be a long journey. I kept an eye out for anything that might dislodge itself from the cliffs—be it falling rocks or winged creatures. My eyes scanned for a place that might enable me to climb out of this valley.

The battle for the mind continued. Every errant thought was uprooted and replaced with another full of hope and promise. I knew I was not alone; there were cloud warriors in this valley. I moved forward, looked up, and trusted.

Something slippery and wet shone in the distance, next to the bend in the river. What looked like two shining snakes lay near the water in the sand at the river's edge. I approached slowly, squinting in the sunlight. As I inched toward them, I noticed they were inanimate. I breathed a heavy sigh of relief.

They were not snakes, but rather two large sticks lying next to one another. One was taller than the other and from its top sprouted multiple short, firm branches. The other—shorter and lighter—lay straight and firm. I picked the larger of the two out of the sand and stood it on end. It looked as if it could support me. I pushed myself into a sitting position and began walking my hands up the miniature trunk. Each pull was agony. I did not care. I could not continue dragging myself around. That would lead me nowhere.

Finally, I rose to my knees. Stick in hand, I grabbed the smaller one and balanced myself. I lifted one foot and placed it on the ground. I was thankful that a lifetime of activity and fitness aided me. My hands and arms did their part. I hoisted myself up onto one leg and gingerly placed the second foot on the ground. It had been days, but I was standing. My new altitude sent a wave of dizziness through me. My breathing became quick and shallow; I slowed it and controlled the rhythm. Slowly in, slowly out—deeper each time. I decided to try a step. I had to begin somewhere, regardless of the consequences.

There were consequences. Pain pulsed through me; my controlled breathing became a panicked pant. I put one foot in front of the other, too stubborn to let pain determine my outcome.

I shuffled down the river on the sandy bank. Now and then I cast my gaze backward, remembering the two diaphanous creatures I had seen there. I wondered where they had gone. The music had been wonderful. I wanted to see them again, wanted to hear the mysterious music and relive the peace that had enfolded me.

They were not visible. The music was gone. My eyes scanned the walls that enclosed me.

✺

The Pathway Out

We, the inpatient population, shuffled and strove to walk. We pushed to increase stride and speed. We pressed toward the mark, leaned into the finish, and worked full-time toward healing (Phil. 3:14). We were united in our efforts to escape the bonds of illness and the incessant circumnavigation of the main desk.

I knew my time for release approached from reading the instructions on the white board. At first it read "dependent" with instruction that I eat nothing. But as the days passed, I graduated to "needs some help." Now the word "independent" glared back at me from the board. I also noticed as the days passed that fewer and fewer people entered my room to take measurements or perform tasks related to my care. They had decided I could move and groove on my own.

Mobility was one standard of release. Mastery of hardware and software were two others. In my case, hardware consisted of the use and changing of the bag. My specialized nurse had visited multiple times to ensure my mastery, or at least theoretical mastery, of the exit ramp.

The software component consisted of the ability to eat and keep food down, and of meticulous adherence to the prescribed diet used to avoid dehydration and disaster. Because every milliliter of fluid intake was measured, they were able to confirm—without a doubt—that a patient was ready for release.

I was well taken care of. I had been visited by an ileostomy coach, dietary coach, visitors from the church, surgeons, nurses, aides, family, friends, flowers, and stuffed animals. I had been left with literature on dieting, the dos and don'ts of certain foods, catalogs of varied ileostomy supplies, websites for further education, and the names of all the wonderful people who had helped me. I was leaving with a supply of hospital socks, boxers, plants, stuffed animals, clothing, and drawstring pants, and with hardware to build up my exit ramp, samples of bandages, bags, and multiple flanges. I'd also received papers, pamphlets, and a full complement of prescriptions for drugs—not as available at home as they were in the hospital. As a grand finale, they had scheduled home visits from a nurse who specialized in the care and feeding of the ileostomy bag. That, more than anything else, provided me solace.

I was leaving with my needs completely met. I was also leaving with a fair amount of trepidation. Having had nurses, medication, food, and any assistance I needed had been a great comfort to me. I wondered if I would be able to fend for myself.

I was not able to walk out. I was forced to wait for the wheelchair—and wait I did, for quite some time. My ride home— who was unhappy about the wasted time in the parking lot—did not respond as positively to the seemingly endless delay. I received a severe scolding about the delay, as if I were solely responsible for hospital policy.

"How come you didn't just walk out?"

I was being yelled at. Welcome back to the real world, I thought.

"Umm, I couldn't walk the distance it took to get to this rotunda." My voice lifted in pitch at the end of the sentence, like I had posed a question.

"I've been waiting forever! What's your problem?"

I'm not sure why, but I decided to suffer in silence. Perhaps it had been my debilitating stay in hospital, or the surgery that had just barely saved my life. And as the drive continued, I wondered what had brought about their outburst. In hindsight, I think my ride was as nervous about my return home as I was.

We traveled in welcome silence. I looked in amazement at the world around me. I had not been   outdoors for weeks. I marveled at the sun, at the people moving freely in their daily lives, completely unaware of the blessing of simple movement. People navigated this outside world frantic with activity, not knowing how much of a blessing this "normal life" truly was. I continued to practice gratitude. I became more and more appreciative of the powerful tool it had proven to be.

We arrived home at last. Challenge number one: I had to get out of the vehicle. It seemed a long way down from way up there in the SUV. My chauffeur came around to my side and supported me the entire way down—a support that would continue miraculously throughout my recuperation.

I was led into the house where a stool was procured to help me into bed. I could not climb the distance onto the mattress. The bed did not rise or lower itself to the floor like my hospital bed. But fortunately, it had an adjustable base that allowed me to maintain the positions of comfort available to me in the hospital.

I crawled in with supervision. I could not turn to reach the end table. Before I knew it, one was jury-rigged beside my bed to accommodate my limited movement. I'd officially entered part one of my at-home recovery. I saw in my future the second operation—the one needed to remove the ileostomy bag and make me "normal" again. But for now, I focused on survival. My thoughts concentrated on my ability or inability to deal with the bag and the pain on my own. I laid my head back to sleep and began, again, the mental battle with fear.

❈

THE DEMON AND THE NET

Darkness loomed overhead. It was time to find shelter. I moved as close to the walls as I could to reduce my vulnerability to attack. Despite my pain and the fear of the unknown, sleep settled upon me.

It was dark—dark and silent. The only audible sound was my breath as it flowed regularly in and out. Slowly, I began to feel pressure increasing on my chest. My body began to struggle as the heaviness increased. Panic overtook me. I pressed against the weight and struggled to rise.

I broke free and tried to run. But my limbs were leaden, and I moved in slow motion. Terror and the need to move faster pressed me from behind, but I was unable to gain distance. My life was in danger—that I knew.

I could not gain speed. I strained forward with death just a misstep away. Help, I cried out in my thoughts. Help!

I began to rise in the air. I had no wings but was still able to direct my altitude and direction. Someone or something was pursuing me. The higher I rose, the more my speed increased. As I jetted forward and upward, blinking stars became visible in the distance. I flew towards them and began to sense my escape.

Slowly, hope dispelled my fears. My body felt lighter. I rose higher. The stars sparkled with my emotions. I breathed a deep sigh, relief pouring through my body. I rocketed upward to meet the stars and smiled.

As I shot upward, I felt the sweep of something close to my feet. Something else was also flying. I strained to rise. I strained to chase the stars, but something seemed to darken and obscure them. As I drew nearer the stars faded—obliterated by something between me and them. It was a net!

The net stretched into a dome above me, obliterating the entire sky. My hope for freedom in this starry night disintegrated. My imminent capture was at hand. I was devastated, terrified. My joy had been an illusion.

My spirit sank into my stomach. The thing at my feet laughed hysterically. The laugh echoed into the darkness and reverberated in the domed net. It pierced into the deep recesses of my body and threatened to stop my beating heart.

The flying, laughing thing scraped its talons against my feet. I strained to gain distance, to escape the lethal claws.

❀

PART 2

The Bag and the Nurse and the Worst

I was released on a Friday afternoon. The visit from my nurse was scheduled for Saturday morning. I was told that it would not be the ileostomy specialist I'd been promised. It was a Saturday after all, and we all know what kind of availability the non-emergent medical community offers on the weekends.

So, I made myself as comfortable as possible and wondered—or more accurately, worried—about changing the ileostomy bag. It was almost overdue for a change. I was beginning to panic because I knew the bag was nearing its last moments of effectiveness, but I gained solace knowing that my nurse would help me in the morning.

Morning arrived. My nurse drove up the driveway right on time. Relief flooded my body and mind. I could not wait for her to help me with the bag change. She completed her various duties: recorded temperature and blood pressure, then looked at the hardware that hung ingloriously from my belly. She took a quick look and said that everything was fine. I was flabbergasted.

"Are you going to help me change this thing?" I asked. "It's already three days old. It needs to be changed."

"You'll be fine." As if speaking to a child, her words stretched out in an unnaturally high pitch. She'd refused my desperate request.

"Fine? I don't think so. This bag needs to be changed. I won't see another nurse for two days. Will you please help me?" I begged her.

"No, you'll be fine." And with that, she breezed out the door. I was shocked. I stood and stared out the window, following her receding car with my astonished gaze. I knew trouble was brewing. Not able to process the fact that my hope had been pinned on a nurse who either had no idea how to manage the bag or had weekend plans that awaited her, I wept. I was on my own with a ticking time bomb hanging from my gut. I knew it could fail and send a cascade of filth down my leg and into my bed at any moment. I prepared for the worst by laying multiple towels under me.

I shuffled back into bed. Every twenty or thirty minutes, I was forced to struggle out of bed to manage the bag. It—this parasitic creature that had become a part of my life—seemed to need more care than a newborn baby. Fortunately, they'd sent me home with medication to manage my stresses. I took advantage of the medication, and in no time I was ready to tuck in for the night.

I awoke suddenly. It was not yet morning, and something was amiss. I had awakened to my most dreaded fear. The bag was leaking onto my clothing. It was a good thing I had placed a towel beneath me. I rose as quickly as my wounded body would allow. Having just been released with a leaky bag, searing pain, and no idea how to deal with it, I broke down. Tears poured out of me, and I fell into full-blown panic mode. Then, from a distant room, I heard the firm voice of my friend call out, "You're tough. You'll figure it out. You can do this."

Those words did more for me than any physical assistance could have. As I stood in the bathroom with filth running down my body and onto the floor, my resolve solidified. I decided then and there that I was going to nail what I'd been taught. I proceeded step-by-step with the techniques. I was new and clumsy but determined. After a grueling thirty minutes, I succeeded with the task at hand and managed to clean myself and my surroundings enough to drag my suffering body back into bed. It had been horribly traumatic. But I felt like a victorious warrior after bloody hand-to-hand combat. I knew then that as much as I hated this horrible process, I was going to be able to conquer it. But I was angry with that thoughtless and cruel nurse.

"I told you. You're tough." That commentary echoed through the hallway as I struggled into my bedroom. I settled into sleep, accompanied by the satisfaction of knowing that I'd won one battle in this war with my body.

The relief was tempered with the knowledge that the war was going be long. My fight had just begun.

Worse Than the Worst

As the week progressed so too did my skill set. There were tricks to this process, and I began to tweak my technique. Visiting angels (in the form of nurses) visited me three times a week. They were specialists whose ministrations were a balm to the soul. I received the help I needed, both technically and emotionally. It was difficult to deal with the physical pain and even harder to reckon with the fact that a part of my body that belonged *inside* was *outside* of me. I gazed at the literal definition of "inside out."

Not only that, but I also watched the bit of small intestine squirm as I dealt with the bag. It possessed a life of its own. Peristalsis took place no matter where the intestine settled. This was a living and breathing thing that protruded from my side. I could not get used to it. One of my greatest fears was the possibility—real or imagined—of having to wear this bag forever. I had agreed to it because my doctor had said it was temporary and would remain for eight to ten weeks. The exit ramp was needed just long enough to give my intestine time to heal.

But what if something went wrong? Any time my mind wandered, I imagined the worst. I had to reign in my thoughts. As I did, I became conscious of the fact that while my body had undertaken the job of healing, my mind had been enlisted into a rigorous training regimen of its own.

I also feared eating. Never in my entire life had I been afraid to eat, unless of course the food was Brussels sprouts or broccoli. I stared at food like it was the enemy. For months—years, even—it had caused me pain to digest anything. My body had become alien to me. My nurse tried to correct my thinking.

"You won't heal if you don't eat."

"I can't eat. Just looking at food makes me sick."

"I'm going to stay right here until you eat every bite in front of you."

She stayed. And true to her word, she encouraged me firmly with every bite. I was reminded of myself as a small child, forced to sit at the table for hours until all my Brussels sprouts were gone. I was creative back then, learning all sorts of places to hide them. I was not given the opportunity to do the same in front of my tenacious overseer.

At the request of my doctor, I was required to go for another test during the second week of my recovery. The thought of having to endure the torture I had experienced with my previous test in the hospital dwarfed any of the fears I had been facing.

Before the test could be accomplished, a good cleansing was required to ensure future pictures could be easily read. I was scheduled to visit my doctor, and I was educated again. There was a method—a shortcut, rather—to the process. Because a bit of my interior hung from my exterior, he was able to flush my intestine out by forcing fluid in through the exterior portion. Sounds like a simple process. And it was—for the doctor. But for me it entailed frequent hurried visits to the ladies' room and thirty minutes of intense cramping. I groaned so loud from the pain that my doctor's voice floated through the door offering help. He was a great doctor, but I cringed at the thought of going through the expulsion process with another audience. Finally, I was pronounced ready for my next day's test.

Trepidation percolated just below the surface of my calm exterior. The brave face I wore into the room lasted only a minute. As soon as the preparations began, all the memories from my previous experience exploded to the surface. This photo session became the single most traumatic, painful moment of my life to date. I was tortured.

THE LET'S CHECK AND SEE ENEMA
OR
PICTURES AT AN EXHIBITION

I waited, unsedated.
Staring at the bag again.
I wept because it tortured me,
it laughed. It knew my end.
It happened that the worst occurred.
Upon my side I lay.
Legs upward bent, my stern exposed,
the nozzle in, was placed.

It did not work. It would not go.
The doctor, he was called.
I lay waiting twenty minutes.
Loudly there, I balled.
The minutes felt like hours
as he took his time, delayed.
I wanted to get up and run,
so far—so far away.

At length, into the room he strode,
and noted my distress.
My eyes were red, the tears streamed down
my tortured, panicked face.
He asked me what the problem was,
I looked into his eye,
"Why have you not sedated me,
I feel like I could die!"

"It shouldn't be that tough," he said.
"We should succeed with ease."
The nozzle in, my gut rebelled,
the barium was squeezed.
With each pump, my gut cried out,
Stop it! Stop it! Ow!
"Move here," they said. "Slide over there.
We need these pictures now."

My flesh cried out, my heart, it broke.
They prodded, pushed, and pumped.
I felt like just a piece of meat
upon the table, dumped.
"Oh God," I cried, "did I just die
and did I land in Hell?"
"Oh no," said they, "you are not dead."
I thought—be just as well.

So there I lay, my belly torn
from outside and within.
The liquid then drained slowly out.
My dignity unhinged.
"The bathroom there, go finish up."
I died another death.
Humiliation covered me
and held me in its grip.

One sink, one towel, one cloth, that's it.
No shower there to use.
I thought I'd not experienced such
disgrace and abuse.

We had finished up the chore.
I limped toward the exit door.
I hunted for the rescue van.
I couldn't step up to get in.
The whole ride home I was afraid
to move. Avoid the mess I'd make.
At home at last, I breathed relief.
Mortified.
Beyond belief.

❁

THE DEMON AND THE
NET (CONT'D)

I strained to fly higher and faster. I stretched to outrun the horror at my heels. I felt the hot breath of its heaving beak, heard the rush of wind as its wings beat the air in vicious pursuit. I strained toward the net and hoped to find a breach. The more I shot toward it, the more solid it became. I knew that if I were to escape this thing I would have to maneuver quickly. I angled my thoughts sharply downward and hoped my body would follow. We engaged in a battle of agility. I knew if the thing caught me in its talons, I would not stand a chance.

Help! I cried out again in my thoughts. I was tiring quickly. The thing turned its talons skyward as it tried to grab me from below. *Help!* I silently cried again.

Suddenly, something—no, two somethings—shot between me and the creature. I felt the wind behind my feet as I strained to escape. As I flew, the sounds of pursuit diminished. I turned and stared. There was a battle unfolding beneath me.

The dark creature fought for its life. Two winged warriors had flown from their chariots and engaged the creature with their weapons. Their swords swirled as they surrounded and attacked my enemy. Their shields buffered them from the onslaught of its mighty beak and talons. Light flew from the tips of their swords as they slashed at the creature. Their swords burned bright with fire, like hot blades from a forge. The creature's screaming reverberated through the air. Its terror and struggle echoed into the night—agonizing cries exploded and shook the air around me.

I watched as the swords of the warriors pierced the demon's breast. As it uttered its final death scream, the net above me disintegrated into thousands of tiny shards. I was free to jet into the stars. I rose higher, turning back for a final glance beneath me. The glowing light of the warriors—and the heat from their fiery swords—melted quietly into the darkness.

Ups and Downs

B ack home again, I battled pain, struggled with the handling
of my hardware, and practiced food management and
experimentation, all of which were unpleasant but tolerable. The
physical governance of my ordeal was beginning to succeed. The
mental and spiritual challenges proved more difficult.

I spent a great deal of energy controlling my thoughts and
emotions. Gratitude and kindness toward others proved to
be powerful tools. But there was a far more primal emotion
that stubbornly refused to submit to my efforts: fear. It lifted
its ugly head over and over. It was tenacious and, despite my
efforts to quell it, became stronger with each appearance. It was
an enemy I knew could be conquered, though I questioned my
battle technique each time it returned. The only thing I found
myself able to do was fight each time it appeared. Some days,
not a minute passed without my confronting it. I knew it could
become like an ignored cancer if I let it grow. And I couldn't let
it metastasize into something deadly.

The thing I feared most was the thought that I would have
to deal with this disgusting bag forever. I could let myself be
carried away by imagination and dread, or—as my wise sister
shared with me, "God does not give grace for what if. He gives
grace for what is."—I could respond with trust. I chose to trust.
I used the promise God had spoken to me on the cruise ship like

a protective shield. I repeated it in my mind and with my voice: "Robin, I will heal you."

Healing was not a steady upward climb. Every day was different. I experienced two steps forward, one step back, three steps forward, two steps back. It was frustrating at times. But despite this back and forth, I was still moving slowly toward health.

As more time passed, I learned how to eat without harming my exit ramp or dehydrating myself. I also began to venture outside my yard. It started with tiny, assisted dizzy steps down the sidewalk. Slowly that developed into independent walks around the block. My confidence began to grow as I built up strength and handled my equipment. Finally, I braved the outside world and went to a restaurant.

It was a new and exciting adventure. But even there I was forced to develop an unpleasant routine. Handling my equipment with skill became a practiced art. Unpleasant public mistakes were made in the process—oversights that forced my immediate retreat back into the sanctuary of my home.

I learned quickly not to trust the thing: the bag. I practiced what I called The Pledge of Allegiance to the Bag. (We stand to place our hands over our hearts to recite the pledge. After a couple of traumatic and panicked misadventures, I began to keep one hand on the bag at all times. It was monitored every minute. I was determined never to undergo that exquisite embarrassment again.)

This kind of vigilance took a great deal of energy. My focus—especially while I was out—was centered on exit ramp management. It was difficult to concentrate on conversation or enjoy my surroundings. To boost my spirit, I was introduced by caring friends to people who had managed this equipment for a lifetime. I was amazed that they were able to perform these tasks with such speed and ease. It was a graphic reminder that dealing with the results of my surgery would not always be as bad for me as it was at the beginning. These angels in disguise were generous with their time and encouragement. I was blessed to have their concern and offers of help. Perspective and gratitude were deployed yet again as I approached my battle of healing with grace.

Moving On

I awoke panting from the dream of my escape. I had run miles in my sleep. My legs were stiff from the exertion of walking the previous day. I forced myself to move. I stood, crutches in place, and stepped out into sunlight. It warmed my body and heart. Hope began to flood my mind with possibility.

The rift in the mountain had remained smooth and wide. Walking became a bit easier than it was the day before. After my muscles loosened, I was able to make faster progress down the canyon. There were short times where I forgot I was in dire straits. It seemed I had time to breathe—to get stronger for the remainder of my journey. I enjoyed the caress of the breeze on my face, the warmth of the sun, and the sound of the stream flowing down the canyon. I had time to think, to try and make sense of all that had happened the past few days. It felt as if I had been walking in two different worlds.

But first I had to deal with the harsh reality of my situation. I was lost, seriously injured, and had no idea how to return home. I'd also experiencing such vivid, otherworldly dreams. Down here in the valley, one reality seemed to superimpose itself upon the other.

As I limped along, I listened for the music that had once filled the canyon. Its tune replayed in my mind over and over. Peace enveloped me as I recalled the gossamer creatures that had assisted me. Even as I fought for survival, I became acutely aware of the beauty that surrounded me. Amidst tribulation there was grace, peace, and hope.

My eyes constantly surveilled the walls that rose above me. They watched for the unexpected. They scanned for a way of escape.

❁

ZIGZAG

The day was warm and pleasant. I walked without hunger and with much less pain than I'd had the previous days. I began to sing in harmony with the pitch of the river as it echoed back and forth. As I sang, I became aware of something in the distance. I cast my gaze at it. Squinting against the light, I saw something in the wall that looked different. Up the canyon wall there appeared a zigzagging line. I shuffled toward it, attempting to reign in any excitement.

As I neared the line, my perspective changed. The stones seemed to open by magic. Behind the edge of a slab of rock there appeared a path. It rose in a mild incline to my right, then it turned around a large rock wall. I strained to see around the bend but could not. I leaned against the canyon wall and considered my options. I could climb it, or I could search for something more accessible. I was feeling stronger, and this was the first possibility of escape from the bottom of the valley I had seen in days. I decided to move up the path when morning arrived.

The sun had disappeared below the rim of the canyon. It was time to bed for the night. Memories of my dreams and hopes for favorable weather in the morning covered me like a blanket as sleep overtook my weary body.

For once it was quiet in dreamland. I awoke energized and excited. Perhaps this was the day I would find my way out. I gathered my pack, had a bite to eat, and stood with the aid of my makeshift crutches. One foot slowly placed in front of the other drew me upward. I was excited; this was the first time I felt like I was making real progress. As I reached the first bend in the trail, trepidation overtook me. I peeked tentatively around the bend. In front of me the trail continued as easily as the first leg. I rejoiced. If I could have jumped for joy, I would have. I exhaled with relief. I hadn't realized that I had been holding my breath.

I moved forward buoyed by the wings of hope. I was cruising now. Compared to my progress of the previous days, I felt as if I was running. I began to relax. I was going to escape. I knew it.

But as I neared the next turn I slowed my pace. The path looked different. The color and quality of stone had changed. Beneath my feet there no longer flowed the smooth, groomed earth. The dirt turned to gravel and the compressed path became deeper sand and dirt. My hands reached out to touch the stones towering above me. They were gritty and slippery. There was a different smell in the air—no longer clean and clear, but heavily earthy. I leaned forward on my crutches and stretched to look around the corner.

My feet slipped from beneath me. I grabbed at the wall of the canyon for balance and a large rock dislodged itself. I pitched forward and fell flat as the rock came down heavily on my injured hip. I lay there stunned, trying not to howl with pain. I thought I was headed home, out of this darkened valley. But now my disappointment flattened me more completely than the painful rock.

From my prone position I stretched to gaze around the corner. An earthy wet smell emanated from the piles of debris that clogged the path up ahead. Heavy rains had washed boulders, dirt, and fallen trees into the path. In my compromised state, climbing over the mountainous pile was impossible. There was no way to crawl beneath it. I was stuck again. I had to return the way I had come.

❋

Almost ...

I spent countless hours resting, reclined and sheltered beneath the blooming branches of my Mulberry tree. It functioned as a restaurant for the entire avian neighborhood. The "Open for Business" sign was posted upon gentle breezes that advertised Good Eating. The birds feasted upon berries while the late spring zephyrs gently caressed new green leaves, brushed over my wounded body, and sang me to sleep.

I started to feel better—normal, almost. I walked some distance, ate some food, did some work, had some fun, swam some laps, wore some of my clothing, and no longer needed nurses. It was perfect, almost.

My fear intensified as the time neared for my deliverance. For me, this meant another surgery, and another stint within the walls of the hospital—a return from where I had come.

As my health improved, the presence of the bag became more intrusive. Earlier, when I was barely able to walk or move, I did not notice the discomfort as much. As time progressed and the portal into my gut began to show signs of wear and tear, the alien on my belly began to leak more of its caustic contents onto my skin. It burned and itched without end. There were times I was tempted to rip the thing off with no concern for the consequences. It happened to be located exactly in the place my clothing should've been. I was not able to wear most of what I owned. Pajamas were not sufficient wardrobe to wear as my previously constricted world increased in size. I began to petition my surgeon to expedite my reconstruction.

He scheduled another colonoscopy to check the junction of the two ends of my intestine that had been reconnected after the removal of the diseased portion. Because the results of my last test had shown constriction, he wanted to guarantee that removal of the bag would cause no complications. He had asked if I would take another "enema test." I flatly refused. That nightmare was too fresh in my mind.

So he mercifully scheduled the colonoscopy. I was put under with Propofol again. As much as I enjoyed drifting into unconsciousness, I was also beginning to feel like Michael Jackson. Never had I been exposed to so much medical attention.

Under I went, and out I came. My first question to my gastroenterologist was, "Can I be repaired?" I waited with bated breath for an answer. I believed my salvation from the bag was dependent upon a positive response from her.

"No," she said. "You are too constricted to repair."

"What can be done?" I whimpered.

"You'll have to undergo another surgery."

She spoke without emotion, matter-of-factly, devoid of mercy. I wept uncontrollably. I saw my future flash before my eyes: one forever attached to the bag. I was overwhelmed.

And another surgery—I couldn't go through that. I was tapped out physically and emotionally. They left me behind the closed curtain for a while. I heard them ask one another what the problem was. "She's shocked at her outcome." I heard it whispered just outside the confines of my curtained space.

It must have taken me twenty minutes to calm down. I was driven home again. This time my countenance hung upon me like the hated bag. I was dejected and without hope.

The next day, I spoke with my doctor. We discussed options. He was a problem solver. In his mind, nothing was impossible.

He had said to me in the past that if he came upon a problem, he could fix it. I loved his confidence.

He gave me three options. One: another surgery. I responded with a resounding, "No." I doubted I would last another operation. His response was to say that perhaps my mind wasn't ready for it, but my body could certainly handle it. He was right—my mind would not go there.

Two: I could get a balloon stretch. They would insert a balloon into the constricted area, inflate it, and stretch the constriction. The risk with this option was the possibility that the intestine would burst. According to him, that was not too big a concern. Because I had a bag, I would not become infected and toxic. It would just require another surgery to repair the repair. "No problem," he said.

Option three: we could "Roto-Rooter" the area to remove scar tissue.

I appreciated the time spent discussing these options. I chose door number two. Despite the possibility of bursting, it seemed the best option.

The three-door option reminded me of a joke my mother told me when I was a younger adult. It involved three doors in hell. The poor soul who had been condemned to this fate was given the choice of one of three doors through which he must pass. He was given the opportunity to press his ear against each door and listen before making his choice.

Through the first he heard loud screaming. Through the second he heard quiet, barely audible moaning. And through the third, he heard the evil laughter of demons torturing their charges. He chose door number two, for he figured it to be less a curse than the other two. The demon granted his request and led him through the second door.

Inside, he saw thousands of people standing for eternity in a deep pool of liquid excrement. It came right up to the pink of their bottom lips. All these people, condemned to eternal ventriloquy, stood still as statues. In voices that did not require the movement of their lips, they intoned, "Don't make waves."

I had been given the opportunity to listen at three doors before I made my choice. I had also chosen door number two. Would my door present a similar outcome?

My surgeon called me the next day. "We have a problem. Your gastroenterologist will not perform the procedure."

"What? Why?"

In the most politically correct, graceful language, he told me that he knew another "gastro guy" who would be more willing to take the risk and perform the procedure—one with similar style and mindset to his own. I wasted no time switching doctors.

The stretch was scheduled, and after another waltz with Propofol, I lay in the post-procedure curtained space and hoped for the best. The assistant entered and delivered the news: the procedure had been a success. I was now cleared for my restorative surgery! I rejoiced as excitedly as a person in my half-drugged state could.

Dismay

With a sore hip, I fought to stand. My stance was low and my spirits were lower. Still, I leaned upon the wall of my prison and stumbled back down the trail that had quite recently offered such hope.

By the time I'd finally arrived at the bottom again, it was time to find a place to rest. I moved forward; the wall of the canyon gave me support as I struggled. I was burdened with more than a pack this time. Hopelessness had taken hold and weighed heavily upon me. I wept openly for the first time in many days. I was careful not to lose control. Panic never helped any situation.

It was cold. I gathered some food and the blanket from my pack. I wrapped myself as I lay down to sleep. The ground felt more unforgiving than it had the past few days. I placed my head upon my pack and settled in for the night.

Morning dawned. I looked down the canyon as far as I could see and saw nothing that afforded me a way out of this side of the river. I would have to cross the flow. After eating, stretching, and gently working out the stiffness in my injured hip, I secured my pack and set off to find a good crossing point where current and depth were minimal.

As the sun's rays found their way to the bottom of the canyon, I approached an area that looked promising. I tested the bottom with my foot to make sure it would support me and my makeshift crutches. From where I stood, it looked favorable. I decided to cross. If the music of this valley had been audible, it would have sounded bubbly and happy on the surface, underlaid with an ominous pedal tone—the harmony of tension and the unknown. And while it was not audible in the air, I felt it resonating in my mind.

I took one step into the water. Then another. It seemed safe enough.

Across the river, reflected on the shining walls, shimmering figures seemed to dance. Perhaps it was just the reflection of water on stone, but they seemed to have form. I took another step. The bottom of the river dropped from beneath me and submerged me. Thankfully, the flow of water was gentle. I struggled toward the surface on the opposite side and saw the shimmering forms more clearly. I recognized the two beings. They had been following me since the beginning of my journey.

They floated toward me. Their glittering light reflected on the water and stone, surrounding me. Time was suspended. I felt the gentle touch of two pairs of hands beneath me, and I was lifted out of the quietly flowing water. They set me on the opposite bank.

CROSSING OVER

I petitioned my surgeon to expedite my restorative surgery. Once again, my doctor—being the attentive, responsive professional he was—came to my rescue. Not more than twenty-four hours after we had spoken, he called with the news that he had rescheduled his roster to accommodate my surgery. He gave me a day to consider his offer. The catch? I would have to reenter the hospital within the week.

I desperately wished to be restored, but again fear had raised its ugly head. If I waited, I knew it could be weeks or months before another offer to proceed. And if I delayed, the alien creature attached to me would remain. As I considered his offer, vivid memories of pain, suffering, and humiliation from my previous surgery assaulted me. A consuming terror enveloped me like a dense fog. Moreover, the joy of swimming in the summer, which helped maintain my equilibrium, would be curtailed. But the idea of having my ileostomy bag attached to me for a day more than necessary drove my decision to agree. There was only one problem: insurance. The decision-makers would have to approve coverage in record time.

I waited apprehensively. I couldn't relax or prepare emotionally. Thanks to my doctor's vigorous encouragement, the insurance company agreed to cover the surgery.

My operation was scheduled for three days later. I was finally going to cross the threshold into restoration. I was going to begin the next phase of my journey.

Barrier

I stood on the opposite shore amazed. I had crossed the river in incredible fashion. I no longer knew what to expect in this valley. The shimmering beings had vanished again. I stood in the warm sun as my clothes dried, and my mind took flight. Peace blanketed me. My hip no longer hurt. I began to walk downriver to search for another possible exit.

The dip under the river had invigorated me. I walked all day. I felt I could go on forever. The sun warmed me, and the sound of the water sang. I combined my voice with the river and the entire valley resonated around me. I listened intently. Then something different began to ring in my ear. Far down the canyon, the sound of running water—quick, tumbling water. As I pressed forward the sound became a roar. It seemed the canyon was narrowing as I progressed.

The source of the cacophony became visible. I had arrived at the edge of an intense cataract. The gentle flow of water had transformed into an impassable torrent that tumbled hundreds of feet downward. Night was falling as fast as the water. I retreated and searched for a place to sleep. Panic descended upon me, and I wondered if I would ever escape.

I found shelter in an alcove not far from the edge of the waterfall. I curled myself deep into it. The soil here was drier, softer. I removed my pack and plucked out some food. The events of the day consumed me as I ate. I'd been lifted miraculously from the waters only to find myself at an impossible dead end. What a strange, wonderful, frightening place this valley was.

My head upon my pack, my body wrapped tightly in my blanket, I pressed as far back against the wall as I could—perhaps to hide from stark realities for a time. Dark thoughts circled in my mind. I cried out for help. I cried from the deepest part of me—for without help, I would not be able to find my way out.

Then I slowed my panicked breathing as best I could, and I prayed for a tranquil sleep.

❁

THE PARADE

As soon as the date was confirmed, fear skulked from the shadows. Like a predator in hiding, it sprang upon me suddenly, clawed at me, and tore apart my practiced discipline. I bled terror. Given that I'd slowly improved, I must have also relaxed my constant vigil. I tried proven techniques to battle my fear, but to no avail. It was as if the monster had silently taken on a life of its own. Undetected within the shadows, it had grown increasingly fiercer and more tenacious.

It stalked me, clawed at my feet and ankles. As I tried to move toward healing, it grabbed me and repeatedly knocked me down. I battled it day and night. I spoke aloud the promise of healing I had received. I read and recited scripture. Still it persisted, dogging me relentlessly.

I wondered: If I could accept the worst outcome imaginable, would it loosen its grip on me? What was the worst that could happen? My surgeon could encounter difficulties during surgery and be unable to restore my body to normal. Or I suppose I could die? Truth be told, I thought the former would be worse than the latter.

For the most part, this strategy succeeded. For a few days at least, fear followed me, albeit too far behind to stab me with its ugly claws or tear at me with its razor-sharp teeth. Was the strategy a mistake? A failure of faith? Perhaps. But from that point on, I felt I was living my last days on earth. A dome of peace and protection steadied atop my head. A quiet stillness enfolded me.

The acceptance of possible death wrought in me an interesting transformation. I saw the world as if for the last time. The Fourth of July was but a day or so away. And while my surgery was scheduled for July 5, I determined I would not miss the town parade scheduled for the holiday. My perception clarified, enlarged, intensified. I saw for the first time the gift of life under a microscope. I saw tiny buds of experience—precious fleeting beauty, the wonder of simplicity—blossom all around me. I went to the parade.

I truly lived that day as if it was my last. The sensation and intensity of the experience intrigued me. I lived without fear. Deep poignancy and quiet joy entwined within me—infused itself into my every breath. My travels through the press of parade celebrants were colored by the unique lens through which I watched.

The parade route was lined with small-town smiles and lollipop-licking little ones. Their ice cream- and soda-stained cheeks declared celebration. Their roly-poly bodies toddled down the street, their sticky hands extended to clasp the hands of protective parents and grandparents. Some were pushed in strollers adorned to reflect the festivity unfolding around them. Some rode upon the shoulders of human horses giving them an alternative view to the sun-touched legs and knees to which they were accustomed. Their parents, decked out in creative—red, white, and blue regalia—chatted, smiled, and pointed out the different fascinations that passed by.

Fife and drum corps and rock bands provided a quick-step marching impetus for veterans, boy scouts, girl scouts, brownies, accomplished teenaged athletes, and members of countless charities and clubs. Shriners donning tasseled hats and police and fire personnel in formal uniform dotted the colorful lines of mini cars, muscle cars, antique cars, and police cars. All reflected careful pride and showmanship. Political hawkers, honking horns, fire engines of all sorts; sounding sirens of multiple pitches, duration, and volumes, accompanied the joyous cacophony. We sweltered together in the ninety-degree humidity, united by pride of country and love of family. We were shining jewels scattered upon the ground.

I returned to my awaiting friends—who had decided not to attend the festivities—to find a beautiful surprise. The friend who had visited me in the hospital during my first stay showed up to greet me and wish me well. They all showered me with tangible gifts of goodness and mercy. These gifts appeared in the form of gracious nurses, homemade food sent by a restaurant-owning friend, someone who took care of my household needs, someone who mowed my lawn, and the visits and prayers of friends.

THE SECOND TIME

The morning of my second surgery arrived. The previous day's peace had fled. I awoke with massive pressure on my chest, crushed by consuming fear. It had descended upon me during the night, and now I was unable to shake it off or wiggle out from beneath it. I felt worse knowing that I'd had a promise of healing spoken to me.

I was ashamed, disappointed with myself.

But the specter of living with the bag forever would not loosen its tenacious grip. Talons of fear, dread, and panic pierced my heart and stomach. I felt their grip tighten around me. Fear overshadowed me, its hungry beak devouring my last bit of control.

Close proximity to imagined death—or worse yet, living forever encumbered by my alien—was the most terrifying circumstance I could imagine. The fear shrieked at me. Its unrelenting noise shook my body, mind, and spirit. It attacked me with such volume that I could not escape its blaring clamor. I felt like the woman in Edvard Munch's *The Scream*. I called my daughter to say goodbye—just in case. But all I could muster was, "Hello. I love you, honey."

I arrived at the hospital, already far too familiar with the routine. The talons of the morning's foul predator had not released their grip. Its wings overshadowed every step I took. I'd had too much experience with the aftermath of surgery to pretend that this one would be the "no problem" procedure promised by my doctor. He had a habit of understating the severity of things. To his credit, his confidence in his skill had buoyed my faith and lessened my fears in the past.

I walked into the waiting room and picked up the Reader's Digest that I knew rested upon the table. As I waited, I took care of my alien's needs—I hoped for the last time. Suddenly, there it was: the call I was dreading, or looking forward to, depending upon the minute.

"Is Robin here?"

My name echoed throughout the waiting area. Yes, Robin is here. I wanted to get going. I wanted to *finish this thing* once and for all. I followed the nurse like a condemned prisoner led to execution. Here was the one and only portal into wholeness and healing—or perhaps the opposite. I breathed deeply and stepped over the threshold.

I was weighed, yet again. This time with no trepidation, for I had lost twenty pounds during my adventure through the valley. Still, I was not out yet.

The intravenous specialist quick-stepped into the room and aimed her large-bore needle at the back of my hand. I panicked and requested that no one touch my hands. Being a professional musician increased my concern about the well-being of my money-making tools. The IV specialist was intrigued, and she asked about my profession. We spoke for a few minutes as she placed the IV into my arm. Then she breezed out the same way she had come in.

I was happy the television worked. I thought perhaps it would divert my attention from dread to more banal things, like the remodeling of homes and gardens. I settled in for the wait, which was scheduled to be no more than twenty minutes or so.

Suddenly, my world was upended—or more accurately, it pivoted on the hurried footsteps of a doctor's mercurial feet.

"Your surgeon is delayed. It'll be about four hours before he's ready to take you in."

Terror seized me. I requested something to modify my anxiety, but the doctor was far too busy to acknowledge my request for calming medication. Off he stalked without another word. I wondered: How can I possibly wait so long with this fear lodged in my stomach? "Oh Father, Help me." I prayed my most succinct and fervent prayer. The next moment an angel of mercy—robed in nurse's clothing—materialized at my bedside.

"Please, can I have something to calm my anxiety? I'm so scared. I've been scared for days. I don't know if I can wait another four hours under this cloud of fear."

"You can reschedule if you'd like."

No. I couldn't. Much preparation had gone into the plan for this day. To reschedule would incur a logistical nightmare and extend my period of limbo for an undetermined amount of time.

"No. I'm here now, and I would prefer to continue with the plan." I was determined to get this over with. "Is there anything you could do for my anxiety while I wait?" I implored.

Her angelic voice said, "Yes. We will help you."

"Thank you so much. I asked the surgeon if he could help, but I don't think he heard me."

"He heard you," she said. She gazed at me with an unspoken understanding and a compassionate look in her merciful eye. She left the room—I guessed to procure one of those miraculous syringes designed to partner with the inserted IV tube. But then she returned and began preparing me to switch rooms.

"Where are we going? Why do we have to move?"

"I have something better for you, but we must put a monitor on you to administer it. There isn't one in this room. So, we've got to move."

We rolled down the hall into a hushed room behind a curtain. The space was set aside for those who needed a bit of extra care prior to surgery. She hooked me up to some very interesting relief. I noticed there was no television to take my mind off the wait.

I shared my concern with her, and she exited the room with a promise to return forthwith.

I waited, occupying my mind with a game I had played in the past: the "let's wait and see if I can tell just when the drug begins to take effect" game. It had just begun to do its job when my nurse returned.

She came bearing gifts. She carried a CD player, a set of headphones, and a stack of classical CDs for me. If I could have risen from my bed, I would have hugged the breath out of her. She had gone above and beyond her duties as a nurse.

"I heard you were a classical musician. I thought you might enjoy these while you wait."

I wept with gratitude. In my eyes, the wings of an angel unfolded from her back, gently lifted her, and held her as she arranged the gifts in usable order. Angels like her had followed me everywhere throughout this ordeal. Nurses—filled with goodness and merciful understanding—had supported me throughout it all. Even as they were pressed by a thousand other necessary tasks.

I perused the selection of music. I was overjoyed. Beethoven was an option. A clandestine visit to a screening of *A Clockwork Orange* in high school had introduced me to his work. I'd become so enthralled with the music that accompanied the violence, I had closed my eyes to listen and missed a good chunk of the movie. I watched eagerly as the credits rolled, determined to discover who'd written the score that had transported me to this previously undiscovered plain. The composer was Beethoven. His music has transfixed me from that day on.

I put the CD in and pressed play. I smiled as Beethoven's rich harmonies and powerful baselines resounded through the headphones into my grateful ear. I smiled peacefully—the music's effect on me was exponentially magnified by the relaxing weightlessness my mystery medication had induced.

A minute—three hours, really—later, she reappeared and announced, "It's time."

"Already?" I mused. I was swept down the hall, drifting upon a cloud of harmony that enfolded me like a cocoon on my journey toward restoration.

THE BANQUET

My desperate cries for help found their mark. I felt myself dissolve deeply into the rock. I seemed to become one with it—or rather I was in it, standing upon it, and beneath it simultaneously.

I could see beyond my shelter. In the distance, golden light caught my attention. I recognized the glow and color of the light that surrounded the chariot warriors. I could see flashing and hear the cacophony of battle. Flanking the entrance into the rock were the two mysterious beings. With their wings extended, they guarded the entrance.

Peace enveloped me like a warm cloud. A gentle hand took my arm, and I was escorted deeper into the rock. I was taken down a narrow passage and deposited before a closed door. As I stood wondering what I should do next, a still small voice from somewhere within me whispered, "Knock." I lifted my hand, knocked, and waited for whatever was on the other side.

The door opened slowly and silently. A large banquet room spread itself before me. In the center of the room rested a massive wooden table. It was covered in a cloth, the colors blue, purple, and scarlet woven into it. Upon the cloth were tableware and goblets of crystal. There was scarlet wine in the goblets, freshly baked bread in the center of the table. The heady scent of the wine and warm bread perfumed the air.

I closed my eyes and inhaled deeply. As I stood at the threshold, I heard another whisper—an invitation: "Enter."

A misty curtain of red swept over the lintel of the door. I stepped through it and over the threshold. High vaulted ceilings drew my eyes upward.

HERE WE GO AGAIN

I entered the operating theater for the second time in two months. By now the blazing lights, superfluity of tableware, and robed doctors and nurses were familiar.

"I'm sorry you had to wait so long," my surgeon said. I did not care at this point. I was happy he'd refused to rush his previous patient's surgery. It meant he would not rush mine. "No problem," I said.

And then the routine began. The anesthetist worked his magic, and again I played the wait and see game to no avail.

The next thing I knew, I was in the recovery room. A bandage on my stomach had replaced the hated alien. This time no Kool-Aid grenade, Nasogastric tube, tubes or bags of any kind decorated my person. I did not even need antibiotics. I was overwhelmed with joy. My doctor had not been exaggerating when he told me that this would be a "no problem procedure."

The next morning came quickly (my surgery had taken place at the end of the previous day). I felt like a new woman. I was energized and felt no pain. I literally sprang out of bed for my prescribed walk. I knew the nurses from my previous stay, and I greeted them with smiles I had not been able to produce the last few months. They commented on how amazed they were by my instantaneous recovery.

But then I began to think. I knew it took about twenty-four hours for the anesthesia to completely leave the body. So I prepared myself for the next day's surprises. I was able to eat, but I limited myself because my intestines had gone to sleep along with everything else during the surgery. I waited for my body to get working again. The hospital would not release me until I was able to utter the magic password: an affirmative response to their probing, uncomfortable inquiries.

While I waited, I stretched out on the sun-drenched couch beneath the window in my room. Southern exposure admitted warm, comforting light. I melted with happiness. The sun spoke to me of hope and health. Light encompassed me and illuminated a bend in the road of my journey. Hope and joy replaced darkness and fear. This sunlit ambiance seemed to foretell of and confirm my bright and healthy future. The promise made to me on the ship had manifested. I could finally rejoice.

I was visited by my surgeon and his colleague. They wanted to ask me questions and answer any I might have. I asked to see my wound, and they obliged. I was shocked to see a gaping, crater-like wound where the loathsome bag had hung just twelve hours prior. It was packed with gauze to absorb fluid. The wound was kept open to allow for drainage and reduce the possibility of infection. According to my surgeon, it would take a month or more for it to close completely. I was also assured that another visiting nurse would be scheduled to help me dress and clean the wound. It didn't matter that my swimming days were over for the summer—I was too thrilled that the bag was gone forever.

Finally, I was able to answer their intrusive questions in the affirmative. "Yes!" I said, stricken by joy. And like that, the magic password opened the door to my release home.

OVER THE THRESHOLD

I'd removed my shoes, dirty as they were from the trail. As I stepped into the room my feet were immersed in a small stream of running water. The water was warm and invigorating. It swirled gently, relieved my fatigue, and washed my feet clean.

I stepped further into the room. My makeshift crutches fell to the ground as my eyes followed the arch of the ceiling. The stone seemed translucent. I stood transfixed. Over the roof of the vaulted space flowed a type of liquid. It enveloped the dome in a shimmering, scarlet curtain.

A voice invited me to sit, and a sense of awe and reverence filled the room. As I approached the table, the deep scent of wine and warm bread—more a sensation than a smell—overwhelmed my senses. My legs weakened, and I dropped to my knees. I felt unworthy to be in this place. "Do I belong here?" I said, looking to the ceiling. The scarlet curtain flew into the room, covering my head and crouching body. I was thankful for this sanctuary, this respite from my pain and worry.

The voice whispered again, "Come to the table."

I did not have the strength to rise. But familiar hands lifted me and brought me to the table. The bread was placed before me, and I ate. It was warm and filling. All the weakness and pain fled from my body.

Then a tiny goblet of the crimson wine appeared in front of me. I drank—first tentatively, then completely. It tasted bitter, then sweet as it passed over my tongue. The tastes and smells expanded within and around me. I was aware of nothing else. The bread, wine, and atmosphere of the room were all I knew.

In my mind's eye there appeared a glowing being who shone like the sun. He was robed in white and girded with a golden belt. The figure lifted a golden vessel from the table and poured the contents of it over my head. Fragrant oil ran through my hair and over my face. The shimmering red curtain exploded upward like a great fountain. I saw through the translucent ceiling thewinged beasts and great birds that had hunted me through the valley. They circled the skies above the room. The explosive fountain overtook them, washing them from the sky.

I had sipped the wine and eaten the bread. I had become one with the room and the presence in it. I lifted my hands and began to sing. And as I did, the rocks vibrated and sang the way they had at the canyon's bottom. The small river at the threshold joined in, gradually growing in volume until we had become a thundering symphony.

I looked up. The translucent ceiling revealed glowing beings that hovered above the chamber. They joined in the music and sang in the most beautiful, harmonious voices I had ever heard. As they sang, the firmament began to glow.

Clouds scattered all the colors of the rainbow. Against a crystalline blue sky, each color glowed more intensely than any I had seen, each painting their own song. Finally, an entire swirling symphony of sound and light resounded in the sky.

The harmonies and melodies were beautifully interwoven with triumphant trumpet fanfares. The rhythms beneath, around, and above me combined and shook my body to its core. The music exploded within me. I thought it would stop my heart.

I seemed to be drawn out of my body—upwards through the translucent ceiling of the room. As I rose, the singing, music, and light engulfed me. I became one with it. I was no longer flesh and blood. Now I was only sound and light.

I glowed and sparkled as I rose into the sky. Laughter burst forth from my lips as I mingled with the firmament. Suddenly it overwhelmed me completely, and I lost consciousness.

Home Again Still Set Apart

At home, I emerged from the car less encumbered and with less difficulty. I compared everything on this leg of the journey to what had happened previously. This kept me focused on gratitude, and I was able to put things into perspective and produce joy and appreciation for the tiny blessings in life. Still, my body had just undergone another invasion. So I retired to my familiar lounge under my cherished tree.

As I rested there, my experiences rewound themselves and played on repeat in my mind. I began to glean the lessons learned. I had changed. A quieter, more pensive me began to emerge: a me exquisitely aware of the plights of others, more apt to count my blessings than my curses.

My thinking became more purposeful. I had time to notice the little details of the world around me, time to see beauty in life's simplest—yet so utterly *not* simple—things. As I reflected on my experiences, I saw that goodness and mercy had followed me in the form of doctors, nurses, and friends. I hadn't just survived— I'd thrived. I could see the blessings that had been with me while I'd labored through the valley. I was never alone.

Beautiful people had saved my life and cared for me while I lay helpless. I appreciated that I could eat and drink without fear or pain. And most of all, I appreciated the hidden gift of a newly renovated intestine.

I became more pliable. Suddenly I could accept problems and face them instead of simply wishing they weren't there. Gratitude had become a habit and a joy. I remembered the glow of endorphins produced by a smile; kindness had become my "drug" of choice.

My thoughts had required intense discipline in the hospital. I knew one's thoughts could affect outcome, but now I had seen the positive difference made during my own journey. "For as he thinketh in his heart, so is he." (King James Version prov. 23:7). Gratitude begat joy. Whining and complaining brought pain and depression.

I'd survived a near-death experience. I had heard about and worshiped God throughout my life, but the journey through the "valley of the shadow of death" had connected me with Him in a way not possible until then. To quote the writer of Job, "I have heard of You by the hearing of the ear, but now my eyes see You."(New King James Version Job 42:5). My eyes had seen His glory.

Nurses came and went as I recovered at home. I followed the progress of my healing with fascination, for I'd never had a gaping wound before. Slowly, miraculously, the wound began to fill. To heal. I watched with wonder and anticipation. As soon as it closed completely, I would be able to swim—my avenue to fitness that had been denied over the past few months.

I was delighted with the easy bandaging and the lack of endless bag-emptying trips to the bathroom. After much experimentation with a diet I'd titled "The Training of the Colon," my plumbing began to work on its own again. My fear of eating diminished. The simple gifts continued to bless me as I recovered.

On a lighter note—the lighter side of my ordeal began to emerge slowly—I enjoyed the new ultra-thin me. I spent time "shopping in my closet." With much smiling I tried on clothes I had not worn in years. I loved it. It was the silver lining that backlit the cloud of illness. Friends said things to me like, "Don't lose any more weight!" or they looked me up and down with quizzical expressions and inquired about my well-being. I didn't care—I was thin again!

As I began to venture more often into the world, the humorous side of my ordeal began to raise its goofy head. Questions were directed at me that caused much discomfort and embarrassment. Everyone I spoke to asked me about the workings of my plumbing. Doctors, nurses, and even acquaintances inquired about the well-being of my internal workings. I have a neighbor who is a nurse, and while I was outside one day, she asked me in a not uncertain language how "things" were. I was taken aback. Who talked like this? I wondered.

The coup de grace occurred one day when I called my primary care physician's office to return a call. I spoke to the nurse there. After confirming my identity, she asked me, without so much as asking how I was, "Have you pooped yet?" What! Who talks like this?

I was embarrassed and angry when I hung up the phone. But as I stood in my kitchen, my elbows propping me up on the counter, I began to think of the multitude of questions that had been directed at me as I healed. I started to laugh. The more I thought about the subject, the more intense my laughter became. This was funny—really funny. I took pen and paper and began to list all the questions I had been asked. Tears—a different kind to which I'd recently been accustomed—began to roll down my face. Suddenly I could see the intense humor embedded within the pain.

I continued laughing. And then I began to write. A poem emerged from my revelry. I dedicated it to my surgeon and read it to him on my next visit. He laughed so hard he almost fell out of his chair. I was delighted to have made his day. After all, he'd saved my life.

QUESTIONS

These days, it's funny. I've been asked
the strangest questions. Barely passed "Hello,"
I hear, "Dear patient, how's your anus feel?"
Or "Hi, we're calling back to see if you have pooped yet."
Seriously?
Or "Are you farting? Are they wet?"
Do I really have to answer that?
Or "You pooped? In bits or fully formed?
With help? Or were they naturally born?"
From Doctors, nurses, friends who care,
the questions come, "How're things down there?"
I know it stems from their concern.
To gauge my health, the facts they learn.
Heard out of context, it'd be rude.
You'd wonder how they could intrude.
"Butt,"
Resultant from procedures done;
concern for Two, rates Num-ber One.

✳

Deliverance

I awakened foggily as if from a dream. On the edge of recall, I lay comfortably, peacefully floating between worlds. Warm sunlight danced upon my face. The breeze's gentle fingers danced through my hair, caressed my skin, and lifted me from my reverie.

I opened my eyes and squinted against the brightness. My pain was gone. I braced myself upon an elbow and looked around in wonder. I was no longer in the valley; I was above it, resting on the rim of the canyon. The roar of water no longer filled my ears. The silence was deafening.

I stood—without my "crutches." They were gone. And as I stepped forward no pain assaulted me. I moved to the rim of the canyon—very carefully this time, lest I slip back into the valley. I could neither see nor hear anything from below. I moved back, not anxious to revisit the place.

This location was foreign to me. The water must have taken me much farther than I had realized. But how had I arrived here? I hadn't climbed out of that valley on my own. I couldn't recall finding a path. The last thing I remembered was falling asleep against the rock on the brink of a deadly cataract.

I stood for a long while in the quiet. Slowly the pictures of a banquet room and the sensations of bread and wine floated to the surface of my mind. Dark recollections returned to me: predatory birds, laser-yellow eyes, evanescent shimmering creatures, armed glowing warriors, and charioteers drawn by powerful cloud horses. I vaguely remembered the colors in the sky that accompanied them. There had also been music—indescribably beautiful and powerful music. Water, stone, and light had hummed and vibrated all around me.

I began to wonder if I had even fallen into the valley. I stood now far from the place I had begun my hike. I thought about my return. I no longer knew how to return, for I did not know where I was. In fact, a return seemed unfathomable. Undesirable, almost.

I felt indescribable joy and peace. I was completely free to go in any direction I chose. There was nowhere I had to go, nowhere I had to be. I needed nothing. I reveled in the feeling, closed my eyes, and let myself drift upon the gentle breezes. Like wings of an angel, they buoyed my thoughts, surrounded me with intuited promise and a foreknowledge of yet undisclosed purpose.

I took a deep breath and opened my eyes. Filled with gratitude and the luxury of time, I turned to walk. The warmth of the sun on my face drew me forward.

BEYOND TIME

Time passed. Eventually my walks increased in length, my wound began to close, and food no longer terrified me. I was still set apart from the world though as my energy had not yet returned.

Under my tree, accompanied by songs of the birds, I rested. Many hours there had freed me from time. Like a monk behind a monastery wall, I was freed from any schedule. There was nowhere I had to go, nowhere I had to be. I tried to remember the last time I'd possessed that kind of freedom. Perhaps in childhood, or even preschool childhood.

I needed nothing. I enjoyed the fading of the world, relished it, reveled in it. I drifted away on the gentle breezes that passed over me. I had time to think, time to put my experience into perspective, and eventually, into words.

I had time. And time has proven to be the greatest luxury of all.

❀

Epilogue

I sat facing an angry gray sea. A tumult of emotion spun within me, lifted me up and down, and tossed me to and fro like the roaring waves pummeling against our sturdy hull. I was overwhelmed. Joy and anguish stood like pillars on either side of me. I stared out the window and through the horizontal rain.

It had been exactly one year since my journey through the valley of the shadow of death had begun. I was both horrified—unable to believe I had lived through the experience with grace—and thankful. I was no longer in the midst of that mysterious and shadowy place. I was thankful that I had been able to rejoin normal life with a new life-altering perspective.

I had been sitting on the same ship in the same space exactly one year earlier. Like me, the ship had been refitted and renewed. A year ago I was unable to eat or drink, barely able to stand or sit, and worried about the lack of function in my intestines. I had known I was profoundly ill. Now I was healthy and whole. Sitting in the same location, I saw in startling detail my before and after.

As each day progressed, my mind returned to the place of struggle I had been exactly one year earlier. Today I sit in a steam bath and swim in paradise. Last year on this exact day, I was lying in a hospital bed in humiliating fashion, unable to perform the most basic functions of life on my own. Today I walk beneath palm trees. Last year I could not put my own feet on the floor. Today I sit with friends. Last year friends sat with me as I nearly escaped death. Today I eat like a king. Last year I ate only with my eyes and imagination.

As the anniversary of my surgery passed, I relived the entire experience. My eyes teared, and I wept openly. I would not wish this experience on anyone, but I am thankful to have been pressed into it and through it. I have been taught things and shown things I would never have learned any other way. Most of all, I came to know my Father in a more intimate and trusting way.

My journey aboard this same ship served as a memorial, a voyage of remembrance. I relived the agony of the past year and revisited the beauty that God had revealed to me through the process. It was a memorial to God's listening ear and to His answer of my prayer for healing. His gracious promise to me all those months ago of "Robin, I will heal you" had come to fruition.

God is faithful and my faith has been fulfilled. Amen.

Glossary

Adagio. (It.) "At ease" or "leisurely"; a movement in slow tempo. (p. 5)

Binary Form. A musical structure consisting of two complementary parts, each normally repeated. (p. 84)

Chromatic. Based on an octave of twelve semitones, a chromatic scale consists of an ascending or descending line of semitones. (p. 155)

Common Tone. A pitch shared by two different keys.

Common Tone Modulation. Movement from one key to another using a single common tone as a pivot point.

Contrapuntal. Using counterpoint; music consisting of two or more melodic strands heard simultaneously. (p. 172)

Crescendo (It.). "Growing"; an instruction to become louder. (p. 182)

Dynamics. The aspect of musical expression resulting from variation in the volume of sound. (p. 227)

Form. The structure, shape, or organizing principle of music. (p. 266)

Gregorian Chant. Melodies from the liturgical repertory that can be traced as far back as the 11ᵗʰ century. Chant contains modal melodic line and flexible rhythm. (p. 306)

Harmonics. The individual pure sounds normally present as part of an ordinary musical tone. They are there because a string or air column can not only be heard as a whole, but also as two halves, three thirds, etc. simultaneously. (p. 322)

Harmonic Series. A sequence of frequencies, musical tones, or pure tones in which each frequency is an integer multiple of a fundamental.

Interval. The distance between two pitches. (p. 364)

Measure. American term equivalent to the English "bar" for the metrical units marked off along the staff by vertical lines. (p. 476)

Meter. An organization of notes in a composition—with respect to time—in such a way that a regular pulse made up of beats can be perceived and the duration of each note can be measured in terms of these beats. (p. 485)

Modulation. In tonal music, the movement out of one key and into another as a continuous musical process. (p. 493)

Pedal point. A sustained or repeated note, usually in the bass, above or around which other parts move.

Perfect interval. [**perfect consonance**]. The interval of an octave, fifth, fourth, unison, or any compound of these. (p. 569)

Pivot. A chord (or note) which has different harmonic (or melodic) functions in two different keys. This property is used to affect a smooth transition from one key to another. (p. 583)

Scale. A sequence of notes in ascending or descending order of pitch. It is long enough to define unambiguously a mode or tonality and begins or ends on the fundamental note of that mode or tonality. (p. 662)

Semitone. Half a tone; the smallest interval of the modern western tonal system. (p. 684)

Set of threes. Refers to a collection of objects classified according to a given rule. (p. 688) Repeated sets of threes produce a rocking or circular feel.

Sotto Voce (It). An indication that a passage is to be played in an undertone, i.e., without emphasis. (p. 713)

Suspended harmonies. In part-writing, a dissonance configuration in which the dissonant or non-harmonic note is tied over from the previous chord (where it occurs in the same part) and resolves by step, usually downwards. (p. 740)

Tempo. The "time" of a musical composition, hence the speed of its performance. (p. 758)

Theme. The musical material on which all or part of a work is based. Usually this term implies a recognizable melody. (p. 762)

Time Signature. A sign or signs placed at the beginning of a composition—after the clef and key signature, or in the course of the composition—to indicate the meter of the ensuing music. (p.766)

Sources:
The Norton/Grove Concise Encyclopedia of Music
W W Norton & Company
Copyright 1988 Macmillan Press Ltd, London

Wikipedia

About the Author

R obin Waite is, by profession, a musician. She has played principal flute in a symphony orchestra, written and recorded her own compositions, taught in various school systems from pre-kindergarten to university level, conducted bands and orchestras, and has a private studio where she teaches flute students.

One day, while sitting on a beautiful back porch in the middle of two thousand acres of forest, she began to write. Words poured out of her—first in poetry, then prose. She thinks in musical terms, hears in musical phrasing and form, and uses the twenty-six letters of the alphabet as if they were part of a chromatic scale.

She found that writing prose worked similarly to writing music. As a result this book was born. She is in the process of writing a novel and a book of poetry.

ACKNOWLEDGMENTS

+ Thanks to my sister Meg Papa for her sharp editing and humorous insights.
+ Thanks to Dan Mulvey, English teacher, editor, and published author extraordinaire.
+ Thanks to Bob Holdsworth, coach and fellow author.
+ Thanks to Christine Gerritt, my friend and analytical beta reader.
+ Thanks to Corinne Blanchette, without whom I may never have found an ending.
+ Thanks to my sister Beth Doyle, editor and Elastigirl, who helped me develop a title.
+ Thanks to my editor Evan, for helping me put the final polish on my book.
+ Thanks to the friends who supported me through my ordeal.
+ Thanks to the doctors and nurses who helped save my life and nurse me back to health.
+ Thanks be to God, who saved my life and gave me the idea for this book in the first place.

CPSIA information can be obtained
at www.ICGtesting.com
Printed in the USA
JSHW030008081122
32778JS00001B/12

9 781956 914528